NEW PUBLIC SPACES

NEW
PUB
SPA

LIC
CES

SARAH GAVENTA

MITCHELL BEAZLEY

First published in Great Britain in 2006 by Mitchell Beazley,
an imprint of Octopus Publishing Group Ltd
2–4 Heron Quays, London E14 4JP
Copyright © Octopus Publishing Group Ltd 2006

ISBN 184533 134 6

A CIP catalogue copy of this book is available
from the British Library
To order this book as a gift or incentive, contact
Mitchell Beazley on 020 7531 8481

Commissioning Editor: Hannah Barnes-Murphy
Senior Editor: Peter Taylor
Executive Art Editor: Sarah Rock
Design: Hoop Design
Production: Gary Hayes
Copy-editor: Emma Clegg
Proofreader: Fran Sandham
Indexer: Sue Farr

Set in Berthold Akzidenz Grotesk

Produced by Toppan Printing Co. (HK) Ltd
Printed and bound in China

CONTENTS

Foreword by John Sorrell

Chairman, CABE

LEFT Piccadilly Gardens Manchester, a neglected space created in the 1960s, was transformed in 2002 by EDAW with over 100 trees, a large lawn, a fountain plaza, and a pavilion designed by Tadao Ando.

Everyone in the world uses public space: as soon as you leave your home and walk into the street, or square, or path outside, you are in a public space. In this sense, the public realm is one of the few services that every single person benefits from: whether rich or poor, young or old.

It is, then, surprising that for such a long time little attention was paid to its quality. Public space was overlooked by many as the "gaps between buildings": the focus was on the object, the building. The space around it was created almost as an afterthought. Often, little attention was paid to the underlying qualities of the landscape. Usually, no thought was given as to how the space would be maintained, or who would pay for this.

In the last few years, however, this attitude has started to change. All over the world, politicians, policy makers, design professionals and the public are rediscovering the fact that iconic buildings, however well designed, do not, on their own, create great towns and cities.

In England, this renewed understanding of the importance of the public realm, and the need to improve its quality, has led to the creation of CABE Space, a unit within CABE (the Commission for Architecture and the Built Environment) that was established in 2003 with funding from government and a remit to champion improvements to urban public spaces.

As champions of better public space, we are delighted to support this book, which brings together some of the most innovative exemplars of this renewed focus on the public realm, from countries all around the world.

By supporting this book, we are not endorsing every aspect of every space that has been included. Creating high quality spaces that are of enduring value can be a complex business. It is a process that may involve planners, designers, managers, maintenance teams, and those who create the activities that bring the space to life – the local community, in its widest sense. Achieving this can be difficult, and often spaces will succeed in some respects more than in others.

In England, we still have a lot to learn. Some of the most beautifully designed new spaces we have created in the last few years are starting to look shabby because they are being poorly looked after. This doesn't have to happen. It is not good enough for designers to claim that maintenance staff can't or won't look after places properly; or maintenance staff to claim that designers create places that are impossible to clean. We need to ensure that places are created and overseen by teams of people with a range of skills, and that as a society we ensure enough money is available to care for the space we all use. Funding the ongoing care of public spaces is often difficult, although, as CABE Space's research demonstrates, there are many different models of doing this successfully – and high quality spaces bring measurable economic benefits.

Many of the most innovative new public spaces are being commissioned and funded by the private sector. Increasingly, developers understand that high quality spaces add value to developments and make them far more desirable to purchasers or tenants. This is to be welcomed. However, we need to guard against a situation in which "public" spaces are only available to certain sections of the public. A space in which children, teenagers, or people with no money to spend are not welcome and accommodated is not truly a public space.

So what is a good public space? Although good spaces are difficult to achieve, in one sense it is surprisingly easy to know when they are successful. A good public space is one that is full of people, a place that tempts those people to slow down, to stop, to chat, or simply to watch the world go by, a place that enriches the lives of those who use it.

"Because inclusion is the name of the game, because health and safety hold such sway, because we live in a contentious society and, as the Japanese say, 'they hammer down the nail that sticks out', it is bloody hard to realize anything of quality in the public realm. This is bad for the public."

Charles Jencks

INTRODUCTION

PREVIOUS PAGE Zhongshan Shipyard Park in China. A new fountain has been designed with references to the riveted steel panels used in ship construction. Water features are popular with children the world over.

LEFT The Hadiqat As-Samah Garden of Forgiveness in Beirut, Lebanon is located on the site of Roman ruins in the centre of the city. The design is by Gustafson Porter. Here, public space is being created to signify a new period of peace and unity.

LEFT This bollard in a street in Ravello, Italy, is created from part of a Roman column, carrying on the Italian tradition of reusing fragments of the past in construction. The result is an attractive and very site-specific feature for this historic town.

THE CHALLENGES ARE UNDENIABLE, but this is an exciting time for the design and creation of new public spaces. Although this book cannot possibly cover the full range of innovative and quality projects being created today, it attempts to give a flavour of the many different spaces being explored, and to look at some of the issues they address and the qualities they demonstrate. *New Public Spaces* is aimed primarily at the layperson rather than the professional practitioner, at those who commission or are involved in public space creation in some way, be it the community, private sector, or local authorities. It doesn't preach a right or wrong approach, or provide a set of rules guaranteed to create a better public space. Instead, it looks at a range of recently created spaces that offer different ways of looking at public space, or just uplift our daily lives.

The case studies in the book are divided into types – as far as traditional definitions can be applied – and include parks and gardens, squares, pavements, trails, a swimming pool, a youth centre, a roadside picnic spot, a bus stop, and even a street hoarding. The projects are inspirational in various ways, suggesting that new public spaces can be anything we want them to be, providing we have the imagination to think more laterally, commit to delivering quality, and continue to develop, support, and maintain them.

A few selection criteria have been applied to the projects included in the book. All the case studies are exterior spaces, open to the public, created in the last five years, and accessible. This is primarily a photo-based survey, so it was vital that the projects could be explained in finished photography rather than just by plans and perspectives. Of course, selection is subjective, but all those included are here because they tackle some of the many issues currently being discussed in public space design. Some are more "successful" than others, some more aesthetically pleasing, some grand, some small-scale, but they all demonstrate a breadth of possibilities.

High-quality, well-designed contemporary spaces are the way forward, and employing and supporting talented design professionals to deliver intelligent, thoughtful designs, and create innovative and exploratory space will add to the success of projects.

So, what are the current issues such spaces address? The problem of maintaining public spaces is a key concern, and is often the main drive behind commissioners opting for the less interesting or demanding solution. The many problems created when lottery-funded building projects appeared with little thought of their running costs and revenue streams have been a costly lesson.

New spaces, therefore, need to be managed and maintained without being an exhausting drain on resources. A mix of public and private funding can help. For example, Kathryn Gustafson cites her

Lurie Garden in Chicago's Millennium Park, where part of the sponsorship budget is set aside for ongoing maintenance, as well as for funding the return of the designers to make any necessary changes once the garden has established itself. In the case of the Green Green Screen in Tokyo, the project became self-funding (and may have even become profitable), as its prominent location attracted lucrative advertising, thanks to the design concept and the chutzpah of the architects involved. The annually produced Serpentine Pavilions in London's Kensington Gardens are sold on to collectors to help cover the costs of the project, and the quality of the Landform Ueda project in Edinburgh won it the Gulbenkian award worth £100,000, half the cost of its creation.

Designing low-maintenance space is an important concern, but this needs to be achieved without making it bland and unappealing. In some cases, where a project is high profile or involves significant planting elements, high-maintenance costs have to be accepted. Significantly, maintenance becomes more of an issue with successful projects, as once a space has been enthusiastically adopted by the public it experiences higher usage than initially expected. Making cost savings from the outset, such as specifying cheap grass that only needs to be replaced by a tougher reinforced version a year later, is a false economy. Short-term thinking isn't possible when commissioning public spaces; you are planning and costing for a project with, hopefully, a lifespan far beyond your own, a fact not lost on the

OPPOSITE In 2003 Stig Andersson of SIA Landscape Architects designed The Charlotte Garden for the courtyard of a residential development in Copenhagen, Denmark. The space is used both by residents and as a new "park" for the general public.

BELOW The Charlotte Garden's dynamic graphic design of organic beds and pathways is planted with perennial grasses whose colours change subtly throughout the year. At night, red spotlights demarcate the pathways and illuminate the trees.

great Victorian park builders, whose parks are still in use today. As landscape architect Bruno Doedens of DS Landscaping says, "When commissioners talk about quality public spaces they often mean the choice of materials; when we talk about quality space we mean its spatial qualities and the quality of the experience it provides."

Safety is another key issue. This is twofold: ensuring that the space and its facilities are safe for the public to use, and creating an environment where people feel safe from attack. The first part is a contentious issue – as we become an increasingly litigious society, commissioners are fearful of being sued. In a social context we often abdicate personal responsibility and act as if we expect to be protected from everything around us –

particularly if it has been "designed" by someone who can then be blamed for any injury we might suffer. You cannot design out all accidents, but you can create a space that pre-empts any kind of interaction, and it is sure to be dull, bland, and uninteresting.

Most designers I have spoken to talk of their frustration with this attitude: Charles Jencks' Landform Ueda is a shrunken version of the original concept because of prevalent fears about people falling down it, despite the lack of evidence that this was a risk, and the fact such problems had never arisen on his larger landforms. Arthur's Seat, the ancient Edinburgh volcano, is a public space that presents far more risks. Numerous other concerns include slippery surfaces, depth of water, and inclines. It was specified

that the cycle path at Westergasfabriek in Amsterdam had to be usable by a heavily pregnant women on a bicycle transporting a bag of potatoes, so the incline was far shallower that the designers had hoped, and the views afforded by a higher position were lost. Bruno Doedens designed Tilla Durieux Park in Berlin with enough of an incline so that people had to exert themselves to, from his perspective, enjoy it more. This is a good point – we cannot treat the public as passive, helpless, unintelligent toddlers. It certainly won't help them to act responsibly and it won't result in public spaces that anyone will want to use.

The higher volume of people using public spaces today helps to prevent them from becoming attractive gathering places for drug users, dealers, gangs of youths, and other undesirables who keep the general public at bay. Decayed and unpopular spaces are much more of a draw to these anti-social people. At Westergasfabriek the most regular visitors are people walking their dogs, and they often report any problems seen to the park management. Dog owners are often factored out of public-space design, as dog mess is seen as a major problem, and is cited by the public as a key reason they may not use a space. Some public spaces are more dog-friendly than others, but this group can always be considered by the provision and enforcement of dog "toilets" or creating dog-free zones within a larger space. As regular users, come rain or shine, they should be involved in the planning stage, and their role as unofficial patrols recognized. Other safety factors include better

lighting and clear paths without high shrubbery or hiding places for muggers, clear views across space, and some official presence or surveillance. The best safety measure of all is a very well-used space, where the numbers of people using it make antisocial behaviour less likely.

Many designers have spoken of their desire to design spaces that are site specific, with a flavour of the region or country in which they are located. Some have spoken with derision of the "Barcelona effect" in the 1980s and 1990s, which saw the creation of many Mediterranean-style public spaces copied from the Catalan region and transported elsewhere, with little relevance. This specificity may be subtle, and is sometimes based on the use of local plants and materials, but can also be about local culture and landscape. In the same way that identikit buildings now spring up in the same form in cities from East to West, it would be a huge missed opportunity if public

spaces were also to become so homogenous.

The role of art in public space is changing. Where once art was an after-thought or add-on to brighten up a scheme, artists are now working with designers and architects from the outset to develop a seamless collaboration, in which the art is site specific and part of the whole design concept. A recent trend that many designers and artists have reported is for briefs to demand that the concept should "reduce crime and vandalism", "attract diverse cultural communities", or "make the visitor feel socially included". All these are valid aims, but are part of a bigger agenda and not the remit of an art or design brief. Such a brief can create a space where these conditions might arise, but no design can guarantee it.

The idea that public art should err on the side of kitsch or be representational – because it is public – and that somehow the public aren't sophisticated enough to accept other types of art, lingers on. Hopefully the days of bronze figures "walking" through our public spaces will soon be long gone, and generally art in public spaces is improving, with the help of those commissioning and funding artworks.

This is a dynamic time to be working in the creation of public spaces. Hopefully the projects shown here are only a tiny fraction of the exciting spaces we will experience and enjoy in the near future.

SQUARES AND PLAZAS

THE MAIN SQUARE OR PLAZA IS
the most recognizable and traditional
civic form of public space. If you think
of the main squares of our towns and
cities, they are usually situated in front
of municipal buildings and mark the
notional centre.

Most civic squares, designed in the
19th to 20th century, were conceived of
as an open area of hard landscaping.
They are traditional spaces for civic
celebration and demonstration, but
were until the last decade
predominantly passive spaces and
empty for the majority of the time. If you
yearn to see an equestrian statue of a
long-forgotten military leader or civic
father then a public square is certainly
the place to look. For the most part
these spaces became shortcuts to work

or play and held more attraction to
tourists than to locals.

However, squares and plazas are
now becoming more animated and are
probably the most intensively utilized
type of public space, especially when
they are inhabited by cafés, bars, and
markets. The return of quality retailing,
from out-of-town shopping malls back
into our city centres, has also played a
part in the regeneration of our squares.
Many have been redesigned to accommodate temporary structures and
events and have been a focus for re-
instilling civic pride in regenerating
cities. Others have been reclaimed from
their most recent role as glorified car
parks by removing the cars and
trafficways that dissected them.

Nick Corbett in his book *Revival of*

PREVIOUS PAGE Brogard Square by
SLA Landscape Architects in
Albertslund near Copenhagen,
Denmark. A restoration of a local square
based on the principle of minimum
intervention with maximum impact or
change.

ABOVE Theatre Square
Schouwbergplein in Rotterdam by West
8 Architects. A former carpark
transformed into a new city square. The
square's surface is a mix of different
textures and materials: wood, steel,
granite, and epoxy denote different
activity areas.

the Square notes the important and complex role these spaces still fulfil: "The city square can provide visual relief and recreational open space within a densely developed area, and can also serve to promote standards in public behaviour. If people are to be aware of the complexity and variety of the society they are part of, and if they are to appreciate notions of civic identity and respect for others, there must be a place where they can occasionally see and experience a diverse cross section of that society … By simply standing in a lively public square, where different age groups and different members of society are gathered together, there is a shared experience that evokes a positive sense of participation." The creation of new squares and plazas now comes with this complex agenda: creating a space that is active and busy and one that the public will want to linger in and enjoy in a variety of ways.

Federation Square in Melbourne is an interesting example because it fulfils both a traditional and contemporary role, creating both a civic focus that was lacking in the city and an active events space surrounded by cultural and leisure destinations such as galleries, shops, and cafés. David Hanna, CEO of the Innovation Economy Advisory Board of the State Government of Victoria calls it "the realization of long-held dreams and the practical culmination of over 100 years of vision and revision to create Melbourne's pre-eminent public space." It was an immense undertaking requiring major political support; the lack or withdrawal of such backing has

been the downfall of many ambitious public-space plans elsewhere. Yet Federation Square is a positive case study. Hanna notes, "A project of this magnitude, importance, and cost can only go forward with political backing. At its best, politics both responds to the needs of the community and leads it. Major projects such as this absolutely require the political will to create, resource, and deliver it consistent with the original vision."

As both an open and built space it is a major new landmark for the city, and an injection of contemporaneity. It has quickly become the civic and cultural centre of Melbourne and an attraction for locals, interstate, and overseas visitors with an estimated (according to the local government of Victoria) 7 million visits per year, far above the predicted 4 million. As a focus of 1000 events annually it makes an important contribution to the local economy, and its high profile helps to promote Melbourne overseas. According to Hanna, "We found having an independent company manage the project for the Government has been valuable in that it opened up the opportunity for more commercial relationships to develop, and operating on a commercial basis meant the project wasn't weighed down with bureaucratic red tape, which can often happen."

Another factor contributing to a success story is ensuring politicians do not involve themselves in design issues, allowing the concept to be completed without compromising it. Some find this hard to do, as nearly every architect and designer I have interviewed mentions. The result is often a weaker, duller, and less imaginative space than planned.

By comparison, the Blue Carpet Square in Newcastle is on a minuscule scale, but it is part of a growing trend to carve out new small squares from converging trafficways and odd corners of parking spaces that pepper our cities. Its role is to create a pleasant passing place and point of rest, a stopping place for people during their journeys through cities to shop or work. These new stopping places are becoming an increasingly common sight, small reclaimed squares that visually give

much back to the city and help create a sense of care, order, and new life.

West 8's Chasse Terrein Square in Breda is rather different, a public plaza whose function is to create a connection between the city, the park, and a major new housing development around it. What is impressive here is that all the parking is located underground (a growing trend in the Netherlands that would be good to see elsewhere), allowing the freedom to create such a large public space and resulting in a far better visual aspect for residents. In most housing developments this space would be full of residents' cars.

BELOW The main square of Ravello in Italy, a traditional space where the church remains the focus and its steps provide informal seating. Cafe seating spills out into the square, which is softened by planting. It is a pedestrianized space, making it perfect too as a play area for children.

OPPOSITE Theatre Square Schouwbergplein in Rotterdam has interactive elements for use by the public, and contains four 35m (115ft) high hydraulic light masts. This console (with a step for children) allows the public to move them up and down, creating what the architects call a "mechanical ballet".

While the Square pulls the area together, it cannot be considered a "destination" as such. When I visited, with the aim of taking photographs that included people (photographs of public space projects without the public make little sense but seem to be the norm), my task proved difficult, as residents had left for work and passers-by were few and far between.

The small USF Square in Bergen, Norway, was created from a former car park. Again, this is a growing trend as cars finally receive less priority in the design of our cities and prime sites that were once devoted to parking are reclaimed for all. Here the harbour frontage was wasted on a car park. It is amazing how many key sites near seafronts, by prime shopping streets, gardens, historic buildings, and rivers were devoted to cars not people. Now USF has a café and terrace and is a natural gathering spot for all ages.

In Stortorget Square in Kalmer, Sweden, the city has bravely decided to buck the trend for busy and programmed squares. Instead it has opted to restore one as a more traditional venue for solemn public events and ceremonies, where its quietness and emptiness are celebrated. This square hasn't been burdened with jolly municipal floral displays and dominating public art, but has been conceived as an artwork in itself. As Adam Caruso of Caruso St John, the project architects, says: "A big city should have room for all types of squares."

In Potsdamer Platz in Berlin the testosterone-driven new architecture has led the designers to create an equally muscular response in the Tilla Durieux Park. Here, the articulated-grass sculpture and monumental see-saws reflect the scale of the huge buildings that surround them. It is called a park, presumably because it is covered in grass, but its location and function are also that of a square, blurring the definitions as uses and materials change. As Bruno Doedens of DS Landscape Architects says, "We are talking about a new kind of space, a combination between a square and a park. Fifty per cent is a hard surface, fifty per cent is green. It works like a square as a meeting point – it has a lot of functions one normally finds in squares but have instead been created in a park." Next to it, the Henrietta Park is a square that is primarily an artwork, a landform in the heart of the city. The interesting touch is, whereas many of our squares are defined by the street furniture that crowds them, here, in order to preserve the sculptural design of the space, such elements are situated around the periphery, allowing the square to be experienced as one whole piece of art.

In Stuttgart, a temporary illumination project in the marketplace by Nimbus is an example of the way visually dull spaces can be animated by installation-based work. No permanent redesign of the square was attempted, but it was still transformed and viewed in a fresh light (literally) by the public who were attracted to use it. Projects like this are good ways to explore what squares can be, to debate and raise awareness and interest in neglected spaces and

ABOVE Specially designed seating for Theatre Square Schouwbergplein in Rotterdam helps create a sense of place and uniqueness and is overtly contemporary. The large scale and length of the benches reflects the scale of the square and lighting masts.

provide low-cost, high-impact transformations. This project also added wit and colour to a square lacking both. The conclusion is that playfulness shouldn't be ruled out as a consideration in public space design.

Nick Corbett sums up the new potential for squares and plazas: "In a global marketplace the image of individual cites is increasingly important. Governments are encouraging city authorities to work with the private sector to invest in urban design and regeneration, and new city squares are providing the focus for this activity." This chapter contains a tiny but heartening cross-section of contemporary squares and plazas whose design offers different approaches, scales, functions, and solutions.

FEDERATION SQUARE
LAB Architecture Studio
Melbourne, Australia (2004)

This AUS$450 million dollar project has created a new civic focus for the city of Melbourne. Strangely, given the intensive 19th-century planning of the city and its rather bourgeois flavour, Melbourne has not had a true public square until now. This addition has created a new cultural centre for the city, fulfilling a long-held ambition to provide an authentic civic destination. The present design is the result of a major international competition which was won by LAB architecture studio and Bates Smart Architects. It is a project that has proved to be an enormous undertaking due to its scale, cost, complexity, and the diversity of its features. It has become highly politicized and the topic of much public debate.

The project is a mix of galleries, cinemas, restaurants, and venues housed in a cluster of cohesively designed buildings. In the centre is the large, irregular 3.8ha (9.4 acre) civic square which forms the focus of the project. The versatile sloping typography, raised planters, and surrounding cafés offer plenty of casual seating for outdoor performances. This space, which can hold 15,000 people, is a formal events venue but also has a traditional role as a permeable, flexible meeting and passing place for workers, visitors, and those on their way to nearby destinations. This lends the space constant dynamism which is enhanced by the flexibility of the design, allowing for an array of uses from large gatherings to more intimate relaxation spaces.

Federation Square began in the mid-1990s with a plan to build a small plaza over the tracks of the former Jolimont railway yard. This yard split the city; its removal has allowed the project to knit back some of the urban fabric. The square acts as a bridge to link with further development to the south, establishing connections with the surrounding riverside landscape.

This has been a unique opportunity to create a new urban square in the heart of an already developed city. Within a year, the planners have successfully recreated the dynamism that has taken centuries to develop in civic squares in the Old World. Its proximity to transport, tourist, and civic facilities has added to its popularity, as demonstrated by the fact that in the first year alone 6 million people visited Federation Square.

OPPOSITE An aerial view shows the scale of the Federation Square project, and its relation to downtown Melbourne and the Yarra river.

TOP Dramatic illumination transforms the square in the evening and adds to its dynamism. The topography of the site – which has a capacity for up to 15,000 people – focuses on a stage area to the south-west, adjacent to a large video screen.

ABOVE The square joins the city centre with the Yarra river and the South Bank development with its restaurants, entertainment venues, casino, shops, and apartments.

RIGHT A view of the main square showing the building facade system. Complex surface geometries create distinct two-dimensional and spatial patterns. The cladding is made of zinc, glass, and sandstone – quarried in Western Australia – whose colours are designed to give a feel of the Australian outback.

LEFT The 2.5m (8ft 2in) bench appears to have been created by peeling back the blue carpet, which reveals the illuminated glass-covered "underlay" beneath.

ABOVE Detail of the stainless-steel and cedar-wood spiral staircase, designed to be read as a simple twisted ribbon, which provides a link to the car parking.

OPPOSITE The Blue Carpet stretches nearly 100m (328ft) and is 20m (66ft) wide, creating a new surface which unites the space. The trees are a mix of oaks, chestnuts and planes. The city's decision to promote the square as a piece of public art did raise expectations which have been hard to meet.

RIGHT Detail showing the blue glass aggregates, which give the square its colour, and a standard cast iron bollard appearing to pierce the carpet.

BLUE CARPET
Thomas Heatherwick Studio
Newcastle, UK (2001)

This new square in Newcastle city centre was created from a nexus of roads and pavements, the aim being to connect these neglected spaces into one special place. The space was pulled together by removing all the road and pavement details and creating a new surface as a focus for the square – the blue carpet – constructed from tiles made from a hard-wearing mix of resin with recycled blue glass aggregates that would be fade-resistant; a concept that took almost four years to develop and to prove its suitability. Bollards and trees appear to poke through the carpet surface, and the carpet seems to overlap the edges of some surrounding buildings.

The area had been treeless, as the city had been systematically removing them from the streets, and an important concern for Heatherwick was to bring trees back into the design – not saplings, but mature specimens such as 40-year-old plane trees. The case for using mature trees was supported by the fact that in the past saplings had had a tendency to be snapped by disgruntled Newcastle United football fans if their team had a bad day.

The benches in the space appear to be constructed from peeled-back sections of the carpet revealing an underlay containing lighting and a space for temporary displays of objects. A twisted ribbon of a spiral staircase was also designed to give access to the car park.

The project demonstrates how ambitions to create innovative, design-led projects can attract substantial funding (in this case from the Arts Council of England) to create a project that a local authority budget alone couldn't realize. The square was the first created in Newcastle for 100 years, and is part of the city's ambitions to promote itself as a tourist destination and a major player in the life and urban culture of the North-East of England.

ABOVE Perspective of the site of the old city of Breda, with the park to the south. The project consists of both hard and green landscaping surrounding and linking the different residential developments.

CHASSE TERREIN
West 8 Landscape Architects
Breda, The Netherlands (2005)

This large 15ha (31 acre) project creates a new square and green landscaping around a new housing development situated between an established park and the city centre of Breda in he Netherlands. The master plan was designed by OMA, with a variety of architects designing separate housing projects on the site (all of which should be completed by 2007). West 8 landscape architects were commissioned to knit together the green spaces around the housing and create a new urban square which crosses the site and takes residents and passers-by through the project, which connects the Vierwindeenstraat with the Chasse single and the Oude Vest of the city.

The focus for this case study is the new urban square which West 8 wanted to be a pure hard landscaping to counterpoint the green landscaping around each housing block. The basic design in shades of grey granite and asphalt is based upon a series of offset triangles (a shape developed from the original parking plan). The effect is graphic and breaks up the large space.

All the parking for residents was created underground, freeing up extra space above ground for additional housing and landscaping. This underground car park also serves customers for the nearby casino and theatre, and shoppers from out of town who park here and walk across the square into town. Hard land-scaping was the only option for this space as earth and planting would have been too heavy a load over the car park. A series of handrails differentiate the areas designated for pedestrians only from the cars entering to park and make deliveries to the theatre and housing – but without creating "roads" and "pavements".

West 8 also created an unusual semi-public space within the atrium of an OMA-designed housing block that borders the square. The surface is scattered with pieces of broken terracotta pots and adds texture to the space; the other material used is Corten steel – both complement the ochre colour of the building's façade. West 8 describe the space as being "like a little painting".

LEFT Plan – the grey triangles indicate the square. The majority of the scheme surrounding the housing blocks consists of planting. To the south is the access to the city, with the church, casino, and new theatre located to the West.

BELOW The square leads from the park past the church to the main shopping area of Breda. The pattern of intersecting triangles helps to break up the sheer mass of the hard landscaping surface. Crossing it are the asphalt cycle paths.

ABOVE The atrium garden was created from broken terracotta pots and corten steel. Pots of plants were also added and residents encouraged to add their own. The design was created to offer two different experiences: one at ground level and one from the open walkways above.

LEFT The text cut into the Corten steel is a poem and a memorial commemorating one of the members of the city Council who supported the project but died before completion.

OPPOSITE TOP The handrail separates pedestrians from bikes and cars. The terracotta pot garden can just be seen in the background. In the entrance to the garden are specially designed bollards/seats which stop people riding or driving into the atrium.

OPPOSITE Young oaks have been planted, which will turn golden in the autumn. The triangle motif is replicated in the basalt-filled beds around them.

BELOW A view towards the city cente. A terrace café is being planned for the square.

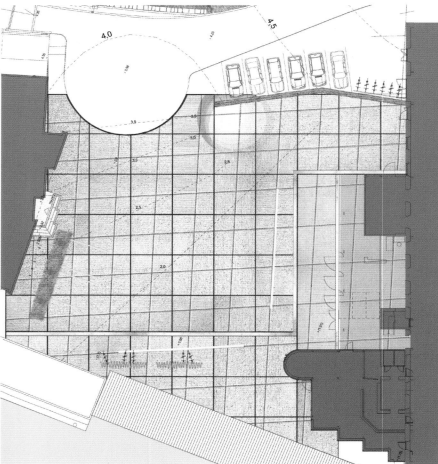

TOP The simple use of cast in-situ concrete creates a distinct slope and a large area suitable for events. The architects created a full-scale mock-up of the design to convince clients that the bump-and-slope technique would work.

LEFT The plan shows the grid-like design, each grid edged in corten steel, the concrete "bump", and the site's location between new-build housing and the cultural centre. Seating has yet to be added to the site.

ABOVE and OPPOSITE
The barrier or bike rack has also proved popular with children as a climbing frame. The rack has a 3cm (1¼in) steel core covered by yellow rubber; locally this material is used to create bumpers around small boats.

USF SQUARE
3RW Architects
Bergen, Norway (2003)

In the Norwegian city of Bergen local architects 3RW have created a new public square from a car park beside the former United Sardine Factory, which was converted into a cultural centre with artist workshops and a restaurant in the 1980s.

The former gravel-covered car park was dusty in summer and full of puddles in winter, and needed a dramatic design rethink. The client (a combination of the cultural centre, a nearby housing project, and the city council of Bergen) come up with an idea of creating a new plaza based on the concept of a steel carpet. 3RW had recently redesigned the ground floor of the cultural centre (adding a glass box to the front to create a wider entrance and more exhibition space) and heard about the scheme for the plaza. They came up with an alternative design based on using concrete. Because of the steep terrain Bergen is full of stepped public spaces, usually constructed from granite. The architects wanted to create a different aesthetic and persuaded the doubtful clients that a sloping surface to the plaza would work as well as steps. Given Norway's climate, this might have seemed risky, but the concrete was cast in situ and literally brushed before it set to create a textured surface that is less slippery in wet or icy weather. Also, heating elements were laid under a section of the concrete to create a clear path in winter down to the entrance of the cultural centre. The concrete was laid out in a regular 5 x 5m (16 x 16ft) grid, each section edged with a Corten steel rim to create dividers and shadow gaps. Fibre optics were set into two glass boxes in the concrete to create interest at night.

Some division was needed to separate the licenced terrace area of the nearby cafe from the square, so the architects decided to create a bright yellow spiral bicycle rack that would function as a barrier and also as a sculpture when empty. The rack consists of two 60m (197ft) long spirals. The square is a both low budget and low-maintenance project that makes a bold and simple addition to the former dock area.

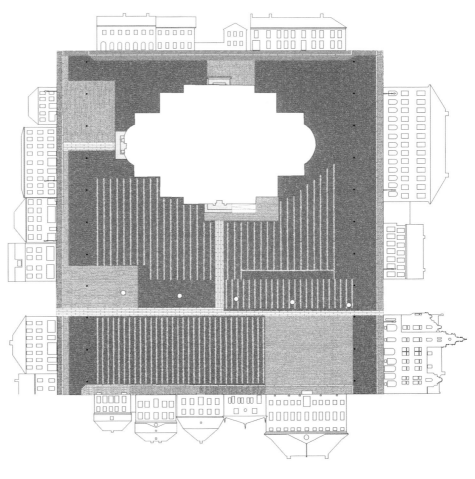

STORTORGET SQUARE
Caruso St John and Eva Lofdahl
Kalmar, Sweden (2003)

British architects Caruso St John worked in collaboration with Swedish artist Eva Lofdahl on the refurbishment of the Stortorget Square around the Kalmar Cathedral in Sweden. This was an unusual, forced marriage in that one of the principal funders selected both the artist and the architect from each of the two invited competition teams.

As it turned out, this partnership worked well because the partners were matched compatibly – an incompatible collaboration could have resulted in disaster. The team worked in synergy to create a concept where the art and design elements were fully integrated in a scheme where the art did not become merely an "add-on" to the urban design concept. For Caruso St John the inclusion of a Swedish team member in Eva Lofdahl also made the various negotiations at local level and the knowledge of Swedish cultural issues much easier to manage.

During its 300-year history Stortorget Square has been a location for political and religious meetings, and a thoroughfare to the shopping lanes nearby. It required refurbishment because the quality of the surface was worn out rather than because of a need to create new functions and facilities for the space.

The first stage was the removal of all the parking spaces, revealing the surface of large stones that have been constantly relaid over hundreds of years. The different stones were laid in patterns, which suggested pathways and routes through the square. Then the granite curbs that had been added to separate cars and pedestrians were removed.

The new design is low impact and low maintenance, and the square's role is that of a space that one passes through rather than lingers in. Yet it is one that can hold enough people for any special temporary events. It is a subtle attempt to give some character back to a space which is empty most of the time; the starkness of the design emphasizes this rather than attempting to make it animated and busy, which would be inappropriate when the space is unused. Since the redesign, the square has received a listed status.

FAR LEFT and **LEFT** The refurbishment has a lightness of touch, with the concept based around the removal of the accumulated years of clutter that dominated the square – such as signage and lamp posts –and the refining and upgrading of the physical surface of the square.

LEFT The square once housed the first well in Kalmar and this history was drawn on by Eva Lofdahl. She created five well-like underground fountains where water passes over a variety of surfaces, such as wooden bowls or sheets of copper, to create different sounds. These are covered by stainless-steel grills that protect visitors, but also reflect the water and the sky.

OPPOSITE Across the square are a series of 6m (3¼ft) high masts on top of which are tiny red lights (actual runway lights). The latter move in the wind, creating a network of light that hovers like a constellation. These red lights have also been added to some of the surrounding buildings.

TILLA DURIEUX PARK

DS Landscape Architects

Berlin, Germany (2003)

In 1995 an international competition for the design of two parks at Potsdamer Platz was won by the Amsterdam-based practice DS Landscape Architects. Their design for the larger of the two parks, the Tilla Durieux, consisted of one simple large intervention, a 450m (492yd) long and 4m (13ft) high grass sculpture turned upon its axis, which dominates the space of this new 2.5ha (6 acre) urban park. This simple and dramatic solution was designed to hold its own against the rather dominating large-scale contemporary architecture that surrounded it.

The park is an open space that is not programmed with events, but is well used by local office workers as an escape from the urban bustle. In the centre are five 20m (65ft) long gigantic over-scaled see-saws: these are bold and sculptural and appeal to young and old alike. Along the perimeter of the park two rows of lime trees have been planted to shield it from the traffic.

The architects were keen to create a space that established a dialogue with the buildings around it, and wanted the slope of the banks to create a physical resistance so that visitors had to exert themselves in order to engage with the space. The architects felt that a little physical effort would create a strong connection between the visitors and the space and that they would therefore remember it more. "Public space should have a character of its own and it has to be extreme, so in order to have an identity it should be more aggressive", says the landscape architect Bruno Doedens.

The simple sculptural design means that even one discarded bottle or newspaper is obvious – so the space does need litter removal every day. Otherwise the park is relatively low maintenance, needing only regular mowing, because there are no planting areas that require tending. Importantly, dogs aren't allowed in the park – this is to encourage people to relax on the grass without any fear of encountering dog mess. Without this restriction the space would fail in its aim to create a lawn for recreation and rest.

The park has a different mood each season: covered in snow in winter it is highly sculptural, in summer it is speckled with sunbathers, whereas in autumn the foggy atmosphere almost creates a seascape.

LEFT The bold design is needed to hold its own against the muscular architecture that surrounds it, including buildings by architects Arato Isozaki, Richard Rogers, and Renzo Piano. The project has been nicknamed the "Dutch Mountain".

OPPOSITE Dorothea Dubrau (City Councillor for Urban Development, Mitte Municipal District, Berlin) is "convinced that this park reflects a future-focused landscape architecture that bridges the gap between contemporary architecture and garden design".

RIGHT The fall of the Berlin Wall in 1989 was the impetus behind the redevelopment of a large area of Berlin where the wall once stood. This included the former Prachtgleis, now the Tilla Durieux Park. The design has to compliment the existing streets around the park.

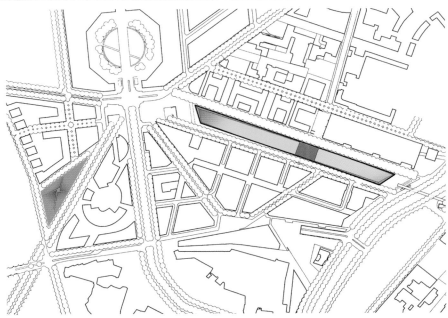

LEFT Part of the reason the project took so long to complete (eight years) was that four rail tracks were built under the park leading to the train station at the end of Potsdamer Platz. A ventilation shaft for the railway had to be incorporated into the design of the park above.

LEFT The giant seesaws were developed by DS Landscape in collaboration with Carolien Oomes from Rotterdam. DS wanted to create some interaction and wonder in the space – these seesaws achieve both.

LEFT A kinetic "wave" effect can be achieved by the seesaws in motion, yet they are equally powerful and sculptural when static. The five seesaws are each 21m (69ft) long and situated in the centre of the park, splitting the grass sculpture in two.

RIGHT The scale of the seesaws encourages strangers to interact and collaborate to create motion. They do not feel like playground equipment, yet do not exclude children. They also appeal to 80 year olds!

ABOVE The seesaw square is paved with cobblestones, creating an East–West crossing point and a more urban hub to the park. The park was named after an Austrian actress famous in Berlin's theatre community. The theatre district was located around the Potsdamer Platz site before the Second World War.

LEFT The park during construction. The grass resembles slightly raised tectonic plates, as if some seismic activity has lifted a lawn. There was no budget for "art", so the fees for working with an artist had to be taken from the main budget.

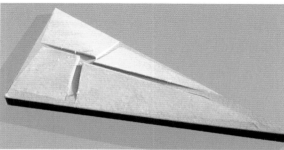

ABOVE The design model of the park, which closely resembles the final project. The broken shards are a metaphor for the division between East and West, appropriately for Berlin. Though broken, the design also suggests these shards could be connected again, a concept which appealed to the city.

ABOVE and LEFT Views of the park showing the Sony Centre designed by American architect Helmut Jahn. Both Sony and the architect were involved in discussions about the development of the design by DS Architects.

HENRIETTE-HERZ PARK
DS Landscape Architects & Shlomo Koren
Berlin, Germany (2002)

This is the smaller of the two parks in Potsdamer Platz designed by DS Landscape Architecture after winning a competition in 1995. The design "Broken Earth" was developed from an idea by the Israeli sculptor Shlomo Koren, the large planes symbolizing broken earth. Koren calls it "an integration of visual art and landscape architecture in one project, fields that are closely related and, at the same time, distant from one another". The artist was involved at the very start of the design process to achieve an integrated approach to art and landscape. The small, 1ha (2.5 acre) scheme was designed to be restrained, to serve as a counterpoint to the more architectural Tilla Durieux park (see pages 40–3) – which is nicknamed the "Dutch mountain" – but both bring land art back into the city.

The design is based upon a broken plate, the shards being a metaphor for the break between East and West in Berlin: broken earth making the tectonic underground forces perceptible. The piece is designed to be walked around or over; the walls are shoulder high, so it feels a little like being in a labyrinth. The robust shards are balanced by being planted with delicate meadow flowers pushing through the grass.

Bruno Doedens from DS Landscape Architects describes it as "a free space that the public deal with in their own way; it doesn't have a direct function or programme and there aren't any rules". Saying that, the rough surface of the paths between the shards has been designed to deter rollerskaters and skateboarders.

To allow the landscape art to remain intact as a scheme, all the necessary elements of street furniture for the park such as benches, bins and lighting were situated around the edge of the space.

The space was named after Henrietta Julie Hertz (1764–1847), who ran a salon that became a meeting place for some the greatest thinkers of the age in Berlin, such as the Humboldt brothers and Ludwig Borne.

As Tobias Woldendorp notes: "Ultimately it does not matter whether it is a park or an artistic approach to public space as long as it finds a place in the heart of the Berliner."

ABOVE and BELOW More than 200,000 Chinodoxa bulbs were imported from the Netherlands to create a carpet of small blue flowers in the spring. The space emphasizes the lines of the streets, the flatness of the land, and the scale of the buildings around it.

RIGHT and FAR RIGHT Raw pink Finnish granite was selected to create the "walls" of the land art. They blend in with the pink gravel selected for the pathways through the artwork. In the winter snow the piece takes on other sculptural qualities.

MARKETPLACE
Nimbus Design
Stuttgart, Germany (2003)

This simple installation project immediately transformed the 6,500 sq m (70,000 sq ft) marketplace in Stuttgart. The effect was created through the imaginative use of lighting, which gave real drama and focus to the square, and demonstrated how crucial a role lighting can play in the presentation of a public space.

The three-month-long temporary lighting installation featured ten oversized (4.5m/15ft high) standard lamps to give a refreshingly new dynamic to what had previously been a rather uninspiring and drab pedestrian square. The lamps create the sense of an outdoor living room, which in itself draws the attention of passers-by, as well as being a theatrical statement.

It is a design concept that Nimbus has repeated in a similar form on other sites in Stuttgart, including a permanent installation at the Romerkastell. Nimbus Design architect Dietrich Brennenstuhl is interested in how problematic public spaces can be brought alive and made more attractive through illumination, helping to create a warmer atmosphere and dispel any sense of a lack of orientation or place. This city-centre market square often used to be deserted at night, but the project has helped to add animation and activity to the square at all times of day.

The installation is interactive, allowing the public to pull a cord and change the colour of the lamps from violet or orange to light green, although they cannot be turned off. The project coincided with the opening of a new bar and restaurant, which gave additional vitality to the space, and has attracted considerably more visitors to the square. The installation ran from October until December 2003, a schedule that also helped to dispel the winter gloom.

The lamps are balanced on large concrete bases, which double up as public seating. Each lamp contains four fluorescent bulbs. The shade is designed from a type of Teflon-coated PES fabric developed by German engineer Werner Sobek, a material that is weather resistant and extremely strong. The posts are constructed from galvanized steel tubing.

OPPOSITE This perspective shows the scale of the lamps, quite literally placing the pedestrian in a giant-size "living room". The base offers both structural stability and visitor seating, while an information panel explains the development of the project.

ABOVE The clustered lights create a focus to the square, which previously lacked any definition. The installation was designed for late autumn/early winter so the illuminations would have maximum effect by brightening the gloomy evenings.

ABOVE (TOP) The colour of the lights can be changed by passers-by pulling the cord, much like with a standard lamp in the average home. Similar lamp-based installations have been used for festivals and exhibitions.

ABOVE A taxi driver reads his newspaper by the light of one of the giant lamps in Stuttgart market square: a touch of home comfort when working the night shift.

"For most of human history streets comfortably accommodated the full range of human activity. In villages, towns, and cities, the streets were the place for socializing, children's play, public meetings, entertainments, demonstrations, and social change. They were also routes for travel and the movement of goods, but until the motor age, there was a balance. Today the balance is lost."

From the Living Streets Manifesto

STREETSCAPES AND PROMENADES

PREVIOUS PAGE The pink granite pavement with its gently scooped drainage channel in the Via Mazzini, one of the main shopping streets of Verona in Italy and also a popular location for an evening stroll. The high-quality, functional design adds to the promenading experience.

LEFT and OPPOSITE The Rolling Bridge designed by Thomas Heatherwick Studio for the Paddington Basin Project, London, in 2004. Both practical and sculptural, the bridge behaves like a woodlouse curled to protect itself. When pedestrians activate it via a button it uncurls to allow them to cross.

OUR STREETS, PATHS, AND TRAVEL routes may not seem at first sight to be public spaces in the traditional sense, and yet these are the most frequently used public spaces in our urban environment. These passages, routes, and simple sidewalks are where most urban dwellers interact with others: meeting and greeting, flirting, waiting for buses, queuing, and chatting on the phone. We generally expect these spaces to offer us very little except a rubbish bin, a place to sit as we wait, or merely a means of getting to our destination.

Streetscapes, bridges, and promenades make up the majority of public space in our cities. Yet, often forgotten or neglected, they tend to be overlooked in favour of squares and parks when answering the challenge of improving the environment. For those of us whose lunchtime consists of a trip to a sandwich shop and back and who don't have immediate access to a major public space at these times, these "passing" spaces should really offer us more. The growing popularity of street café culture, even in northern climates, proves that we are willing to sit on busy, noisy, and smelly streets to watch the world go by, be seen, or enjoy our coffee alfresco – even if the air isn't always that fresh. Yet it tends to be the private commercial sector who respond to this natural desire rather than our local government or councils. When it is not commercially led it is often the local community – utterly fed up with their depressing street environments or routeways – who initiates this type of project.

As pavements become wider due to traffic-calming measures, there are more opportunities to create real public

spaces on some of our streets. The same is true of pedestrian walkways. At one time the underpass was a dank place that was best avoided or travelled through at great speed; now many are being transformed into brighter, cleaner, and more pleasant thoroughfares. As more of us walk and cycle through our cities, either to work or to get fit, quality promenades and cycleways become more important. If our governments want to encourage us to become fitter, then more pleasant public spaces in which to do this are vital. If such improvements to our everyday environment are a source of pleasure, then perhaps we may be encouraged to use our cars less for short journeys. And if these routes are diverted away from traffic lanes and instead hug our rivers and green spaces they will give us the opportunity to enjoy our cities more.

Tiny areas of asphalt or broken paving stones in combination with some bollards and municipal seating may result in small and inconsequential spaces. However, they can make our day-to-day existence more pleasurable as we perch there to make a telephone call or eat a sandwich. These are the dead public spaces of our cities – we can all think of some we pass daily that could be transformed by additional elements and a bit of imagination, such as new paving, planting, seating, lighting, or art or design features.

The projects in this chapter suggest that the possibilities for this type of public space are endless, based on imaginative responses and the creation of new definitions. They need not all be highly expensive, as a small-scale addition can make a large-scale impact in such an environment.

LEFT A decorative yet contemporary pivoting steel fence designed by S333 Architecture and Urbanism to separate the residential courtyard of their Schots 1 and 2 project in Groningen in the Netherlands. The design is based on reeds growing in the nearby water basin. A standardized fence could have been specified, but the architects decided to create incorporate specific local references to add design quality to its function.

The projects are tremendously diverse. For example, an art-based street-furniture project in Tokyo elevates street furniture into sculptural elements; leading international designers, artists, and architects were commissioned to create a series of permanent installations that have transformed the landscape of a pavement. It demonstrates that many types of practitioners are capable of producing this kind of work, all with equally impressive results. The design concepts range from creating outdoor room sets – almost outdoor living rooms – to art works that can be sat upon, and over-scale street furniture. What they have in common is that they engage and attract the public.

In Teural, Spain, the architects have created a dramatic walkway through the city walls, which is a piece of sculpture in its own right and restored a traffic-clogged square, giving it back to pedestrians to enjoy again, responding to the Spanish culture's love of the *paseo*, or evening promenade. The memorial bridge in Rijeka, Croatia, is on a route that takes shoppers from the main shopping street to the car park on the other side of the river; but it is also a landmark, a memorial, a place for contemplation and one that allows pedestrians a fresh view of the city and the river.

In Zutphen, in the Netherlands, the subtle upgrading of the pavement materials and redesigning of shop boundaries, combined with new lighting and street furniture, has transformed some rather run-down streets into a far more attractive shopping experience. This has even attracted new businesses as a result. Quality environments do affect our behaviour and responses, and these small changes have had a far bigger effect on this small historic town. They give an instant feeling that the local authority cares, and this sense of optimism and renewal has influenced visitors' perceptions of the town.

The Eastern Esplanade in Portland, Oregon, is an almost curated journey, with the very pavements and lighting providing visitors with information on the location's history. The cycle and walkway give an intimate experience of the river and a peaceful, almost rural, journey in a urban context. This moment of peace and quiet is what many of us hanker after in our urban life. It isn't the same as experiencing "nature" (although that appeals too), as this calm experience can equally be offered by a promenade as by a park.

In San Candido, Italy, an intriguing solution has been found to deal with the ebb and flow of people in spaces, both the quiet and busy moments, so that even when empty there is no feeling of desertion or lack of activity. The new spaces for the town bring quality elements, which knit together the town's streetscapes. The vital factor that makes this project successful is the removal of traffic from the centre – but unlike similar pedestrianization schemes of the 1960s the programme of animation, even when empty, has ensured that these new public spaces do not have the bleakness associated with schemes such as the South Bank in London and the resulting fear of crime.

The Liffy boardwalk in Dublin is a simple yet effective idea. This project takes the promenade away from the edge of the traffic and creates a pedestrian boardwalk that literally hangs over the edge of the river, sheltering the public from the noise, fumes, and exposure of the street. In this way a necessary journey is turned into a pleasurable experience that may even encourage you to linger on. This scheme has been so successful that it is being extended along the river.

Greyworld, a group of sound artists in the UK, accept the physical limitations of our urban realm, but aim to bring another dimension based on a combination of sound and wit. If you can make the army of gloomy faced, trudging commuters actually smile on their way to work then this provides an excellent alternative approach to animating our experience of the environment. Why shouldn't railings be musical as well as

functional? Then you could run your umbrella along them as you hurry along and enjoy the resulting sounds. And why can't the surface of an urban bridge recreate the sound of an autumnal woodland path? The sound of crunching leaves or fresh crispy snow has the potential to transport you to a far more stimulating environment, even if only momentarily.

One of the problems with these types of spaces has been that when they were created by road-department planners or architects they were viewed as simply the access ways to new buildings or transportation hubs, and their role as public space wasn't considered.

Many transformations are a retro-fitting exercise, as the designer Thomas Heatherwick knows too well. He is often called upon to create a sense of a special place in areas that have no character or distinction – from the roundabouts of the A13, to the pavements outside the International Stadium in Manchester, to his Rolling Bridge at the Paddington Basin in London. The Rolling Bridge is a spectacle as well as a walkway; it curls up like a woodlouse protecting itself and uncurls when called upon to function. Heatherwick's frustration is that designers aren't brought in early enough when these spaces are first conceived and therefore have to add something "special to them later" instead of designing a quality public space to begin with.

I believe these small overlooked spaces are where we should focus our attention, rather than concentrating on showcase parks and squares which,

OPPOSITE ABOVE and BELOW Ertunc Enver, a graduate of Goldsmith's Ecology and Design BA course in London, created this public space communication system for the blind and partially sighted. The different tactile finishes on the paving stones can be felt when walking, indicating the presence nearby of useful street elements such as a public phone booth, seating, or bus stops, as well as obstacles such as rubbish bins, trees, etc. It can be retrofitted into existing paving.

although important, do not impact on our lives to the same extent as the regular journeys we make between home, work, and leisure. If the creation of a quality urban environment is about knitting together the spaces left over from the regeneration of our cities, then these "in-between" spaces are the final darning that is needed to make this transformation complete. They require innovative and imaginative approaches and solutions, as there are many restrictions and considerations necessary, but they are often low cost in proportion to their high use and the impact and value they can add, enhancing our daily experience of the built environment.

ABOVE Designed by Hibino Katsuhiko, this piece, entitled "Where did this big stone come from? Where does this river flow into? Where am I going to?" was inspired by the memory of the River Nagara in the artist's hometown of the same name.

THE ROPPONGI HILLS PROJECT
Various designers and artists
Tokyo, Japan (2003)

Locals regard Roppongi Hills as a large-scale contemporary version of the *monzenmachi* or "quarters before the gates". These amusement districts throughout Tokyo provide visitors with a place to rest and be entertained. The Roppongi Hills project took a total of 14 years to plan and three years to construct. It occupies over 11 ha (27 acres) and has created a new cultural centre for Tokyo.

Around the Mori Arts Centre, the Mori Art Museum, and the Roppongi Hills Academy is a diverse community. The area includes new offices, luxury residential high-rises, a cinema complex, a performance-art arena, and the broadcast headquarters of TV Asahi and J-Wave Radio. In addition to these facillities there are gardens and more than 200 shops and restaurants.

Within the area is a wide variety of public art and street furniture – commissioned from international artists, architects, and designers – has been integrated into the new urban landscape. These works include Louise Bourgeois's gargantuan spider, positioned at the base of the Mori Tower, and looming over passers-by; Cai Guo-Qiang's rock mountain which landmarks one of the street corners; and Tatsuo Miyajima's oversized digital counter which adorns the outside wall of the TV Asahi Building.

There are also 11 benches and a bus stop dotted along a 400m (1312ft) stretch of the main street in Roppongi Hills, Keyaki-zaka Dori. Designers include Andrea Ranzi, Ettore Sottsas, Droog Design, Ron Arad, Jasper Morrison, Tokujin Yoshioka, Thomas Sandell, Karim Rashid, Shigeru Uchida, Toyo Ito, and Katsuhiko Hibino.

The pieces are fun and thought-provoking, providing users with a space for relaxation and interaction.

Four of the works were chosen by David Elliott, the director of the Mori Art Museum, and a further three works were selected by architect Fumihiko Maki for installation in and around his TV Asahi building. Each piece of street furniture is very different, with an overall emphasis on achieving a diversity of colour, form, material, and inspiration.

LEFT Isa Genzken's 8m (26ft) high "Rose" towers above the Hollywood Plaza in the north-west section of Roppongi Hills. Various architects have created buildings around the tall flower – these include offices, cinemas, and shops.

BELOW Andrea Branzi's "Arch" simultaneously appears as a cross-section of an interior (with table, chair, and light fitting), a window, and a piece of street furniture. The rectilinear frame allows the concept of "inside" and "outside" to change constantly.

RIGHT Park bench by designer Jasper Morrison – a typically restrained approach by the designer. Simple and well-designed, the bench can seat 20 people. Cypress slats were used to blend in with the surroundings and mellow over time.

ABOVE Another view of Andrea Branzi's "Arch" along the main street in Roppongi Hills: an interior juxtaposed on the side of a busy road.

OPPOSITE (TOP) Visitors taking a break on the giant Corian pebbles designed by Thomas Sandell. These are scattered in front of Miyajima Tatsuo's "Counter Void" which forms part of the wall of the TV Asahi Building, designed by architect Maki Fumihiko.

OPPOSITE (BOTTOM) Passers-by are silhouetted against Miyajima Tatsuo's "Counter Void". On the 50m (164ft) long wall six illuminated neon panels repeatedly count down from nine to zero at different speeds; the numerals glow by day and the background glows at night.

ABOVE "Evergreen" by Ron Arad incorporates 24 bronze tubes covered in ivy. The perpetual loops that the tubes form represent the endlessness of nature. Over time the ivy will continue to grow over the framework, eventually covering it completely.

RIGHT "Day-tripper" by Jurgen Bey for Droog Design is inspired by the various poses that people assume during the day while they are seated. It is constructed from polyurethane foam, covered with glass-reinforced polyester, and printed with a traditional Dutch silkscreen flower pattern.

PASEO DEL OVALO
David Chipperfield Architects and b720 Arquitectura
Teural, Spain (2003)

The Paseo del Ovalo is an historic promenade in Teural built above the old city walls. One of a number of historically sensitive monuments in this world-heritage city, the Paseo del Ovalo has a strong Moorish heritage with Moorish towers dating from the 9th century.

The project involved the redesign of the public route from the main railway station up to the historic promenade. The original access was solely via the huge staircase, so lift

access from the Plaza Estacion below to the Paseo del Ovado was needed.

Teural is rather an isolated city, keen to become a popular tourist destination, and the imminent arrival of a high-speed train service linking it to the rest of Spain prompted considerable competition for the project. The winning architects, David Chipperfield Architects and b720 Arquitectura, convinced the decision-makers by coming up

with a plan to perforate the wall, instead of using an external lift which would have involved adding a structure to the outside of the wall. Now, users who do not want to climb the huge Mudejar-style steps leading to the Paseo can follow a path to a 15m (49ft) tall contemporary designed cavity within the city wall. This leads them to a lift lobby, top-lit via the glazed lift shaft that follows through to the upper level.

The interior is lined with Corten steel, and the rusting steel surface is illuminated by sunken uplighters. In the Paseo above, parking spaces and a petrol station were relocated, the road redirected, and traffic-calming measures introduced. This space is lined with cafés, hosts fiestas, and is popular

with locals. The lift entrance here was designed from glass and matt stainless steel so that it was low maintenance and wasn't too obtrusive in the square. The same palette of materials, including grey pavers and black concrete benches, connect the two spaces. A careful and modest approach to the design ensured that the historic qualities of the original space weren't destroyed, but the project has also added a high-quality contemporary landmark to the city. The project won The European Prize for Public Urban Space organized by Barcelona's Centre for Contemporary Culture in 2004.

ABOVE An overview of the Plaza de Estación with the new "cave". The low wall on the left is illuminated at night and provides a boundary for the public space. The Neo-Mudejar staircase dates from 1910 and was restored as part of the project.

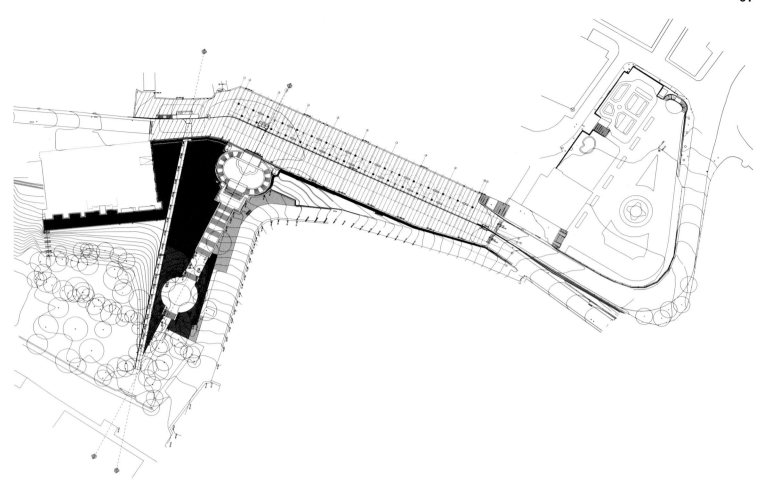

ABOVE Plan showing the new path running diagonally to the existing steps, with the areas of refurbishment highlighted in grey. Despite being called the Paseo del Ovalo (meaning the oval walk) this description refers to a former fortification and the Paseo itself is rectangular in shape.

RIGHT View showing the two routes to the Paseo above. The wall leading to the lift entrance is only a temporary fence. The new path is constructed from local white limestone and is described by the architects as a white carpet beckoning you towards the cave.

ABOVE and TOP Interior views of the lift entrance or "cave". Sunken uplighters add to the sense of drama in the space.

LEFT The new entrance has been cut into the wall but remains flush to the wall, and the hinged stainless-steel door is closed at night. The huge cavity dips down to a more human-scale entrance, but expands out again once inside.

OPPOSITE The Paseo del Ovalo, showing the new glass-brick entrance and, on the other side of the road, the Neo-Mudejar staircase. The views are over the new part of the city, towards the river and railway station below.

MEMORIAL BRIDGE
3LHD Architects

Rijeka, Croatia (2004)

The Memorial Bridge is a 47m (154ft) long public space, a pedestrian bridge that is also symbolic: it was designed to commemorate the Croatian soldiers killed in the Balkan wars, many of whom embarked for war on buses near the site of the bridge. It is a place of memory as well as social interaction.

The brief called for a bridge and a memorial, but the architects decided to make the bridge part of the memorial too.

Funders initially thought the design was too simple and abstract, desiring a more Soviet-realist style complete with heroic figures.

The bridge is located in the centre of the city over a canal that separates the historic city centre from a car park, which will become a city park or business district in the future. The memorial is L-shaped, comprising the horizontal of the bridge itself with two vertical monoliths, which mark the end

of the bridge, and contrast with the empty, open car-park space behind them.

Every part of the bridge and memorial monoliths was made off-site, then assembled on-site. The 150 ton steel construction of the super slim bridge (it is only 65cm/25in thick) was produced at a local shipyard and floated on a barge to its location.

Marko Dabrovic, a partner at 3LHD architects, describes the design: "Our response to the task was to create a bridge as monument, to visualize the utilitarian and symbolic function, construction and forms. The structure consists of two archetypal elements – a plank laid over the canal as a bridge and slab driven into the earth as the monument.

Symbolic emphasis is accomplished by a cleft in the vertical element, and a red memorial slab in the cleft extension. In other words, the task we set ourselves was to make a structure that would dominate the area, while at the same time awakening an intimate feeling – that is, to create a monument for walking."

The result is a dramatic yet simple solution which the visitor or passer-by can engage with at a range of levels, aesthetic, practical, or emotional. It has achieved its aim of being both functional and symbolic – a difficult task for such an emotive kind of project.

OPPOSITE The monoliths and bridge looking towards the historic area of Rijeka.

ABOVE These three images show the process of construction and floating the bridge on a specially designed barge to its location. The barge was designed so it could dip beneath the low existing bridges.

RIGHT A view of the sides of the monoliths, which were constructed from a pre-cast concrete core covered with aluminium and specially made glass bricks from Slovenia. A machine in the top of the monolith emits an intermittent high-pitched sound, only perceptible to birds, designed to scare away seagulls to stop them from soiling the memorial.

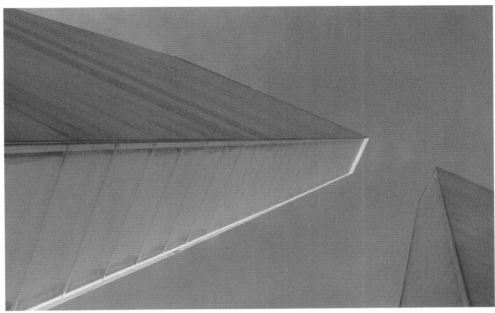

LEFT The location of the bridge is at the end of the main shopping and promenading street in the city. The bridge extends this promenade over the water and provides access to the temporary car park site. Its L-shaped design can be clearly seen in this aerial photograph.

LEFT The stainless steel and teak benches on the car park side of the water were also designed with an L-shaped profile. There are hidden LED lights underneath the benches to illuminate them. They have become a popular location for sun bathing and picnicking.

BELOW Appearing almost like a shadow of the monolith, a 1m (3ft) wide strip provides the formal memorial space. The benches cast similar shadows to echo the memorial.

OPPOSITE TOP and BOTTOM The bridge is illuminated at night by concealed LED lights situated beneath the teak handrails, casting a glow over the whole surface. The bridge has become a place of civic pride, and has not suffered from any vandalism.

RIGHT This formal memorial site can be walked across. It is designed as a place to leave tokens of remembrance such as flowers and candles.

BELOW The surface decking of the bridge is constructed from aluminium and was made in Sweden. The only text on the memorial is cut out of the surface of the decking.

LEFT Crushed bricks (symbolizing the earth) laid into concrete have been covered with epoxy resin to create an unusual surface. The narrow gap between the standing monoliths that people can pass through was designed to make visitors fully aware of the experience of engaging with the memorial.

BELOW A daylight view from the benches on the car park side of the memorial.

ABOVE A view of the aluminium surface of the bridge with the commemorative text running across. It translates simply as "Croation Defenders' Bridge".

ZUTPHEN STREET IMPROVEMENTS
Okra Landscape Architects
Zutphen, The Netherlands (1998–2005)

The masterplan for the project in Zutphen aimed to upgrade the heavily deteriorated streets and public spaces of this small Dutch town. This involved reclaiming the space in the historic centre from its domination by traffic and improving the pavements and street surfaces.

The main shopping area is called *t'rondje* by the locals. The streets are laid out in a winding medieval pattern and this forms the heart of Zutphen.

From the Middle Ages the streets and alleyways were characterized by individual pavements in front of each building, each with their own stoop, or verandah area. In the 1970s these were all replaced with a uniform layer of low-grade concrete, but this had deteriorated badly. It was only recently that enough civic funds were available to undertake a quality refurbishment on this scale.

The shops have been given Belgian limestone edging and attention has been paid to the connections between the various streets and alleyways so that they merge into one another. Okra, the landscape architects, removed signage poles and the glass shop extensions and window boxes that had appeared over the years. They also set all the electricity boxes underground along with the other services.

The improvements appear subtle, but the effects have been dramatic. Formerly ugly streets with run-down and closed shops have been appropriated by new businesses, and are now flourishing. The town itself is attracting affluent residents who commute to other areas.

The pedestrianization of the market and town-hall squares has enabled café terraces to flourish and allow the organization of events, and the use of these areas, once again, as informal meeting places. The improved market facilities (with plug-in access to below-ground electricity and water) have attracted so many more vendors that the market has actually grown, a great indicator of a thriving commercial centre.

This project was supported through three local administrations in the city, demonstrating the long-term aspirations, commitment, and planning by both the city council and the landscape architects.

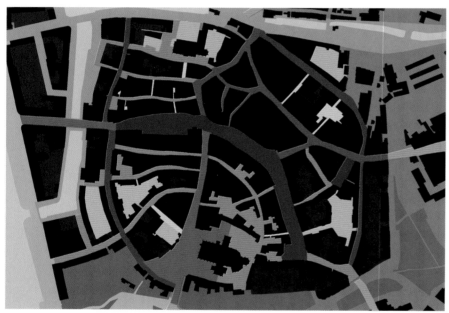

ABOVE Plan of the centre of Zutphen, showing the major shopping streets and squares. Those in the darkest blue have already been refurbished, and the plan will soon be extended to the other highlighted streets and squares.

RIGHT Layouts of the Belgian limestone edging, brick pavement and their relationship to the street. Special attention has been paid to the connections between the various streets and alleyways so that they merge into one another.

ABOVE Lange hofstaat, one of the main shopping streets. The appearance of the meandering shopping streets has been greatly improved by the laying of new street and pavement surfaces, the removal of obtrusive street signage, and the burial of electricity and other services underground.

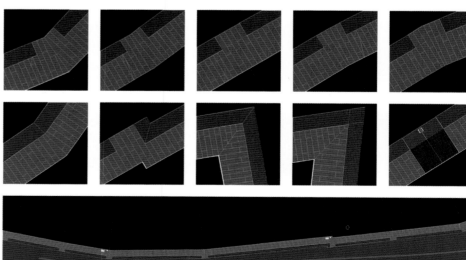

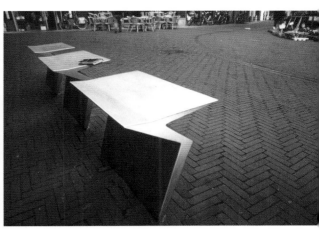

ABOVE Folded and polished high-grade steel has been used to create new street furniture – this contrasts with the other natural materials used in the development, and reflects light. The seats can be used from all sides and there is room for two people to sit on each one. The stools are filled with sand so they cannot be used as makeshift "drums".

LEFT and BELOW LEFT The Belgian limestone edging widens around corners, and changes in the direction of the paving denote boundaries between the shops. The colour spectrum of the illuminated shop windows is reflected in the pavement. The material adopts the colour of its surroundings and becomes an integral part of it.

BELOW Gentle, indirect, wall-hung lighting illuminates the medieval buildings. The former lampposts were removed as they were obstructive in such narrow streets. The contemporary design caused controversy, as a faux-traditional style had been seen as the obvious approach, but this design is successful because of its simplicity and unobtrusiveness.

RIGHT Overview of the Esplanade, looking north. The Esplanade links a number of unique pedestrian spaces along the River Wilmette as it flows through downtown Portland. Riverbank restoration work used bio-engineering methods to stabilize the riverbank and create a fish-friendly habitat.

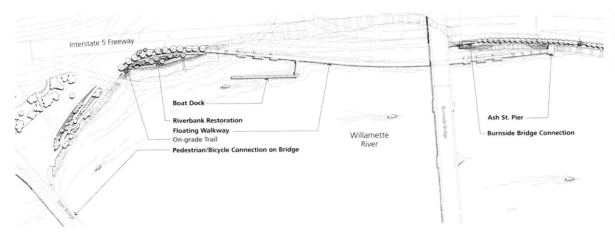

Interstate 5 Freeway

Boat Dock
Riverbank Restoration
Floating Walkway
On-grade Trail
Pedestrian/Bicycle Connection on Bridge

Willamette River

Burnside Bridge

Ash St. Pier
Burnside Bridge Connection

LEFT These plans of the north and south ends of the Eastbank Esplanade show certain features – such as riverbank restorations and bicycle paths – designed to harmonize the development with its riverside environment.

Eastbank Esplanade - North End

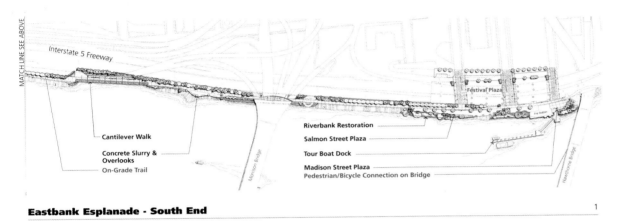

MATCH LINE SEE ABOVE

Interstate 5 Freeway

Cantilever Walk

Concrete Slurry & Overlooks
On-Grade Trail

Morrison Bridge

Riverbank Restoration
Salmon Street Plaza
Tour Boat Dock
Madison Street Plaza
Pedestrian/Bicycle Connection on Bridge

Festival Plaza

Fire Station

Hawthorne Bridge

Eastbank Esplanade - South End

1

EASTBANK ESPLANADE
Mayer Reed Landscape Architects
Portland, USA (2001)

The Eastbank Esplanade is part of a 5km (3 mile) pedestrian link along the Wilmetter River in downtown Portland. It runs for 2.5km (1½ miles), extending from the Hawthorne Bridge to the Steel Bridge, with connections to the Eastside residential neighbourhoods as well as across the river. The project features a floating walkway, a promenade, plazas, viewing places, lighting, planting, moorage, and public art. It is fully accessible by bike, on foot, or by wheelchair.

Designed by Mayer Reed Landscape Architects, there are 13 "urban markers" at key locations along the Esplanade that mark the city's street grid. Mayer Reed, who have an in-house graphics department, designed 22 interpretive panels providing information about the river and the rich history of the area, from the building of the city's bridges to the development of Portland's Eastside. This aspect of the project provides the visitor with

a curated journey, as you might receive in a galley environment, and makes the Esplanade a cultural and tourist destination as well as a leisure area, adding an additional level of experience and understanding.

The 366m (1200ft) floating walkway is the longest of its kind in the USA, with the adjoining public dock providing moorage for recreational boats and a space for a future river taxi service. The construction of the Esplanade was carefully timed to be sensitive to fish-migration seasons, and several large "root wads" were brought from central Oregon and anchored in place along the riverbank to provide important habitat areas for fish. The restoration of the riverbank included planting 280 trees and over 40,000 shrubs.

The "looping" shape of the Esplanade provides an easy connection between the east and west side of the centre of the city. It has become the location for many events, including firework displays, kayaking trips to explore the river bank, bike trips to look at nature in the city, photography workshops, lectures, and an urban fair – all part of a programme run by the city's Parks Department.

74

LEFT The floating walkway provides a trail connection where the bank disappears under the freeway. The walkway accommodates a river fluctuation of over 9m (30ft) seasonally.

ABOVE RIGHT The walkway is constructed of concrete and steel, with a total of 65 pylons, each of which is embedded 9m (30ft) into the riverbed. Sections were constructed in Bellingham, Washington and then trucked to the site and floated into position.

RIGHT The white caps on the floating-walkway pylons are designed to discourage birds from landing on them and hence reduce the problems of bird droppings falling on the walkway – or passing pedestrians and cyclists!

RIGHT and FAR RIGHT Each 6m (20ft) high stainless-steel marker includes corresponding local street names to re-establish the park's connection to the city, from which it is separated by a freeway. The markers also contain interpretive panels and lighting.

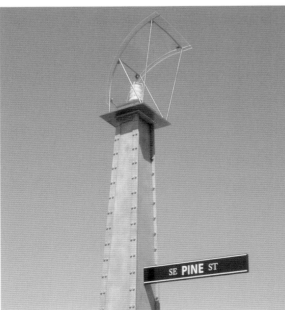

FUZI PEDESTRIAN ZONE
AllesWirdGut (AWG)

Innichen/San Candido, Italy (2002)

Located in the Upper Puster Valley in the South Tyrol and in close proximity to the Dolomites, Innichen (also known as San Candido) is a popular tourist town with 3000 inhabitants. The requirement was to redesign and increase its pedestrian zone (a project named "Fuzi") to take account of the seasonal influx of tourists. A competition was launched to find a design that best achieved this. The winners were Viennese

architects AllesWirdGut (which translates as "everything will be fine").

Due to the town's fluctuating tourist numbers (it is most popular during the skiing season), the old zone was overcrowded during peak periods and deserted and forlorn during the low season. The new Fuzi project consisted of five zones: the main shopping street, the main square, a church square, a functional events space, and

a small park. The architects created areas that could change depending on the season and number of users: for example, boardwalks that work as terraces for cafés in the summer and which convert to street-level flowerbeds in the quieter spring and autumn. Greater flexibility is gained by using slightly sloping areas that can be flooded with water to create mini-ponds and fountains to break up the scale of the large open spaces, thereby adapting it to the reduced number of visitors in the low season.

Most of the light sources are hidden. In the main square the building facades serve as reflectors, while in the shopping street the light is reflected from the pale street

surface. By illuminating the façades, the form of the main square is defined, highlighting historic details and strengthening the overall spatial character.

The design concept means that the various connected zones can easily be modified for different uses and numbers of people. They have been designed to be animated in a lively, aesthetically coherent, and intelligent way that requires a minimum of restructuring. These open spaces of the zone act as a showcase for the town.

LEFT The lightsources are hidden, with the illuminations being provided indirectly. The light intensity decreases upwards so that the artificial light does not compete with the natural.

BELOW A model and plan of the interconnected spaces of the Fuzi pedestrian zone. One of the main aims of the project was to reduce the amount of traffic in the centre of the town and convert these spaces into pedestrian zones.

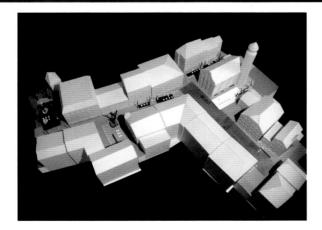

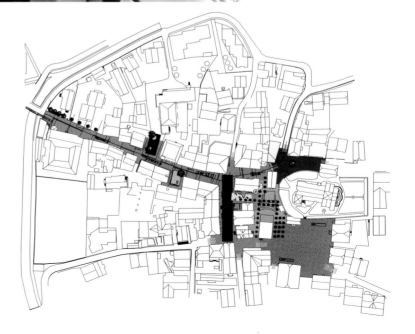

ABOVE and LEFT At night (above) and during the day (left) the raised terrace area is illuminated from underneath so that it appears to float above the square.

RIGHT Even in daylight the globe-shaped illuminations make interesting features juxtaposed with the surrounding trees.

BELOW View from Michaelsplatz to the Dolomite mountains beyond. In the foreground is one of the new ponds, designed to add interest to the space at times of the year when there are few tourists.

LEFT Illuminated globes create interest in the intimate park space. The gravel comes from a local quarry and reflects the colours of the nearby Dolomite mountains.

BELOW The platform in Michaelsplatz was conceived as an illuminated terrace. The cafe seating is moveable to enable customers to follow the direction of the sun.

LEFT The fountain can be turned off and the water drained to provide additional terrace space during high season.

ABOVE and BELOW AllesWirdGut developed a piece of street furniture that combined a bench, lighting fixture, and noticeboard from black pre-cast concrete, and also designed additional concealed lighting and sunken bicycle stands. These features are planned to reduce the amount of clutter normally visible on most urban streetscapes.

LEFT A fountain – and paddling space enjoyed by a young resident – converted from the existing surface of green serpentine that covers the square.

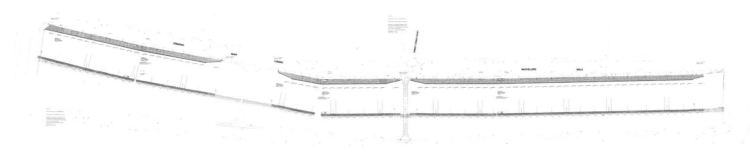

ABOVE A plan of Liffy Boardwalk, demonstrating the way it hugs and turns to follow the changing course of the river.

ABOVE The Liffy Boardwalk at night, showing the wide wooden rails, the lighting that leans towards the deck, and the way the boardwalk separates pedestrians from the heavy traffic of the road running parallel.

LIFFY BOARDWALK
McGarry NiEanaigh Architects
Dublin, Ireland (2000)

This new boardwalk was the idea of Dublin City Council's chief architect, Jim Barrett. The concept was to create a pleasant pedestrian route away from the cramped pavements and traffic chaos of the quays, the roads that run either side of the River Liffy.

The 650m (2132ft) long boardwalk was situated on the north quay so that its south-facing direction would provide a sunny relaxation spot for Dubliners. The structural solution consists of a system of propped cantilever frames tied to a series of diagonal rock anchors situated well below the existing footpath and the buried cabling services in the street above. The boardwalk level is much lower than the street, and this helps to muffle the traffic noise and allows sloping disabled access. The lower level also takes into account the potential flooding risks and the scale of the passing river traffic.

The architects McGarry NiEanaigh decided on a simple vocabulary of materials that already feature along the River Liffy, including painted steel railings and wooden decking. A major feature of the boardwalk is the benches, the largest being 70m (230ft) long. The boardwalk rail is designed to be leant upon and coffee stalls have sprung up along the boardwalk, making it a destination as well as a new pedestrian route.

The boardwalk has given Dubliners a new engagement with the river, from which previously they were separated by the high granite quay walls. As the river itself bends sharply along the route, so does the boardwalk, creating junctions that become natural viewing points. The project has become a characteristic city landmark, appearing in numerous advertisements and films, and the volume of users has far exceeded expectations. On the basis of this success a second phase was completed in 2004, adding another 240m (787ft) to the project.

RIGHT The decking turns into a ramp to allow wheelchair access.

BELOW RIGHT View showing one of the large wooden benches with the coffee stall directly behind it.

BELOW LEFT This shot clearly shows one of the key characteristics of the boardwalk, which changes direction as it hugs the wall and flows around the bend in the river.

STREETSCAPES AND PROMENADES

"Creating a park for dummies doesn't work; you cannot use a standard checklist but need to think creatively, work in fresh ways, bring in expertise, and take some time."

Evert Verhagen, Project Manager, Westergasfabriek

GARDENS AND PARKS

PARKS AND GARDENS HAVE A HIGH popularity ranking for public spaces, and it is true that a quality park or garden can have a massive impact on its city or neighbourhood, influencing property prices and general perceptions of an area. The great urban parks of the Victorian era – the lungs of the industrial cities – suffered a lengthy period of neglect and decline in the second half of the 20th century when cutbacks in public spending resulted in poor maintenance and security, leading to many becoming no-go areas. Public authorities often removed many of the traditional park elements such as bandstands, fountains, tearooms, and pavilions as they were costly to maintain and were prone to vandalism. By 1994, in Britain alone, less that 10 per cent of parks had cafés or kiosks and only 25 per cent still had public toilets, making them less than attractive venues for an afternoon out. The municipal floral displays beloved of Victorian and Edwardian park design, such as floral clocks and carpet bedding, were labour intensive and expensive, and disap-peared from many parks from the 1960s onwards. The beds were turned over to low-cost, low-visual-impact shrubbery or lawns, creating rather bleak land-scapes. There is an "urban-park myth" that in every major park in Britain is buried the rusting mechanism of a floral clock.

This decline of our parks and gardens is, thankfully, being reversed in most cities, and today green space that is well cared for gives urban dwellers a much-needed connection with nature. Surveys indicate that the urban population of England alone makes 2.5 billion visits a year to a green space. Along with a revival of our historic parks and the creation of new ones, there is also a resurgence in garden creation and design, both public and private. According to Penelope Hill, a critic specializing in contemporary landscape design, "Until recently there had been no radical break from the past in modern garden design, as witnessed in art and architecture. Its vocabulary, theory, and form belonged to previous eras, with only a few designers attempting to break with tradition in favour of innovation. It owes its regeneration to a wide range of influences, the most obvious being developments in the arts and science, modern communications, education and ecology, architecture and urban design, and the historical and social changes that have altered the face of Europe over the past hundred years."

She also raises a valid point about the way in which we judge whether these new design approaches create parks and gardens that really work. "Gardens must stand the test of time if they are to be enjoyed by subsequent generations; they must withstand the elements, allow for growth, remain adaptable, and fulfil their function if they are to be cherished in years to come."

To the general public, attractive public space equals green, and nature and green always seems to equal good, even though a neglected balding grass lawn covered in litter and dog mess has to be one of the most depressing sights

PREVIOUS PAGE Please walk on the grass – an image from a promotional campaign by CABE suggesting an new attitude of increasing accessibility in our parks and garden. The public are now encouraged to appropriate and interact with the spaces instead of being simply bystanders kept to the paths.

OPPOSITE A temporary garden installation designed by architect Richard Eisenmann within the grounds of the Castelvecchio in Verona, Italy, shows a dramatic contemporary sculptural approach that works well in the historic surroundings.

in a public space. However, new design approaches don't always result in the creation of green parks and gardens. The projects in this chapter demonstrate this new definition. Some are traditional in type but not execution, some are more architectural or sculptural, and others aren't green at all.

The South Eastern Coastal Park by FOA in Barcelona, for example, is primarily a hard-landscaping project, the main design element consisting of concrete crescent-moon-shaped tiles with minimal planting and trees.

The Millennium Park in Chicago is an example of how much parks have been socially rehabilitated to the extent that

they now attract rich private and corporate sponsors, in the way that an art gallery or opera house would have done in the past. Every element here has a sponsor, from the Lurie Garden and the Pritzker Pavilion to the BP Bridge. Again, traditional park elements such as water features, pavilions, and gardens have been updated – the only shame is that this contemporary vision wasn't applied to the boulevards and spaces that link the major elements. Here, classical stone-effect balustrades strike a twee note, a compromise that lets down the ambitions and boldness of the project as a whole. The park has been incredibly popular with the public,

LEFT Contemporary public seating for St James Park in Clerkenwell, London, designed by students from Goldsmith's BA Design course. Each steel-backed seat is punched with a different image of a person relaxing, reading, kissing, or eating on the bench. Its high back affords a rare chance for some privacy in a public space.

OPPOSITE The public gardens in front of the town hall in Ravello, Italy, consist of a simple yet colourful display of pansies, which are pleasant for passers-by and visitors.

in part due to its prominent location on Michigan Avenue. It has no real boundaries, either, so it spills out onto the street and draws in passers-by who may not have planned a visit. This lack of boundary makes it very unlike a traditional park. The outdoor café turns into an ice rink in winter and you cannot help but be drawn in by the buzz and fun of the place, even if the walkways fail to meet your aesthetic expectations.

Charles Jencks' Landform Ueda project outside the Gallery of Modern Art in Edinburgh demonstrates, like the Serpentine Pavilion project, the effect such a public space project can have on visitor numbers. The Serpentine reports an extra 200,000 visitors to each pavilion, while the Gallery of Modern Art can only confirm that on the Family Fun Day, which took place around the Landform in May 2003, visitors to the gallery increased by 145 per cent. Can it be just proximity to the public space

that made the gallery such a draw? Presumably, it is also about the level of enjoyment that public space affords, as a pleasant experience may encourage you to seek another, or perhaps you just popped into the galley to use the lavatory or the café and decided to check it out.

Whatever the reason, it has a quantifiable effect. In an age when galleries compete for funds based on the increases in visitor numbers (and new visitors) they achieve, then the public parks and gardens they commission around them can play a vital role.

Dania Park in Copenhagen is a stunning piece of contemporary landscape design, of which there seems to be plenty in Sweden. A seaside park – a type rarely seen in Britain – it is the first major park created in the city for 40 years. Thorbjorn Andersson, the landscape designer responsible for the project, feels if it had been designed 40 or 20 years ago it would have been very different. If it was 40 years ago the emphasis would have been on planting, and 20 years ago it would have had a more ecological, naturalistic theme. Today, however, the approach is far more architectural. To create a successful project of this nature, Andersson believes that firstly you need an engaged client; secondly, the parks should be designed as spaces where people can be themselves, arenas for social inclusion, and where everyone has an equal right to be.

The Anchor Park, also in Copenhagen, is unusual in that it is designed to become overgrown. It factors in and welcomes decay with its overtly organic shape and its emphasis on ecological considerations, and creates self-sustaining eco systems that help reduce maintenance work.

Columbine Gardens is included in this chapter for one simple reason – flowers. To find a contemporary garden where the design is based on flowers is a rare find, as flowers have fallen out of fashion – odd given that gardening is an increasingly popular pastime and florists really do flourish. True, flowers require maintenance, dead-heading, and replanting to keep displays fresh, but they also provide an extremely uplifting experience for the visitor both visually and aurally. Wild flowers have been returning as a feature of gardens, as seen in the Millennium Park in Chicago, but bold intense graphic planting has long gone. Flowers and

municipal aesthetics can be a rather scary combination, a display in Minehead in Somerset based on the theme of clotted cream teas will stay etched in my memory for ever. But even so, these are popular with the public and can be wonderful in the hands of a designer such as Stig Andersson of SLA in Sweden, who designed Anchor Park and whose work is very graphic in design. Adriaan Gueze of West 8 feels it will be at least another 10 years before designers will move away from hard landscaping and architectural outdoor-room approaches towards more floral solutions in park and garden design. His new Lebas Park in

Lille does attempt to engage with this issue in a limited way by creating formal flower beds that burst from the lawns onto the pathways. Gueze also believes that tackling the design of parks requires considerable experience and that the designer should be mature, rather like the space they are creating, because of the particular longevity of this typology – he himself, a great park lover, just feels ready to tackle such projects.

The New York Restoration Project set up by the actress Bette Midler is an inspiring story about how committed individuals can help turn around and restore a dying park such as Swindler

BELOW The floral beds of J D Lebas Park in Lille, France, by West 8 Architects. The flowerbeds extend out of the lawn into the hard surface of the pathways.

ABOVE Contemporary public seating for St Johns Park, Britton Street, London. The oak bench is a modern rethink of the traditional wooden park bench, with a dip in the seat to accommodate children or a place to rest one's lunch.

ABOVE RIGHT A bed of nails constructed from tightly packed traditional park railings, also in St Johns Park. Both this seat and the wooden bench demonstrate the effect quality seating elements can bring to a park or garden.

Cove Park in New York and attract sponsorship and support. The NYRP is an impressive charity that has transformed many neglected parks, disused lots, and overgrown gardens in the city, rather than leaving them to an overstretched public authority to manage. They are practical, imaginative, and passionate. The bag snatcher, designed to grab plastic carrier bags caught high in trees, invented by Bette Midler's husband, is a great, simple idea that sums up their hands-on approach. They involve the local community in their work, and this local ownership and participation is an important factor in helping to create and maintain successful parks and gardens.

Many new parks that are being created today are located on former industrial or commerical sites, and two such parks, Westergasfabriek and Zhongshan Shipyard Park, are case studies in the next chapter, "New Uses For Old Spaces". Parks like these have an additional quality due to their transformation. They are both a new park amenity for each city and a reminder of its industrial past containing structures from its former life

adapted to create new and unique design elements. These are parks that are also partly heritage sites and outdoor museums. They illustrate the continuing potential and changing design and definition of parks and garden spaces.

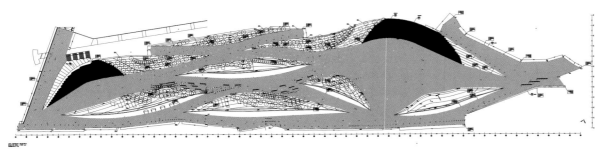

ABOVE Plan showing the layout of the artificial dunes in the South Eastern Coastal Park, which sweep over and cover the site and run parallel to the coastline.

SOUTH EASTERN COASTAL PARK
Foreign Office Architects (FOA)
Barcelona, Spain (2004)

The 50,000 sq m (59,800 sq yd) South Eastern Coastal Park in Barcelona is an enormous outdoor performance space consisting of two auditoriums. It was planned to host large-scale rock concerts and was part of a major scheme for the area for UNESCO's Forum 2004, which includes projects by Herzog & de Meuron and Abalos & Herreros.

The site has an 11.5m (38ft) drop from the main esplanade to the shore, and Foreign Office Architects (FOA) developed a design that bridges the level difference.

The main requirement was that the park should be accessible to vehicular as well as pedestrian traffic so that heavy equipment for concerts could be brought onto the site. In order to avoid earth being ploughed up by wheels and the creation of a muddy surface, it was decided that the whole space should be composed of hard landscaping rather than grass. To shelter visitors from the sea breezes a series of artificial dunes were created; these have an additional function to provide three "burrows" to act as storage for furniture and lighting and to be used as cafés.

The main construction element is the bold crescent-moon-shaped concrete tiles, designed to be strong enough to withstand the weight of trucks passing over them. The size was limited by the weight, which was no more than the weight that could be carried by two workers. Their shape allows the flexibility to lay them around planting and drainage points, as they can adapt to different lines and geometries, and they have also been used vertically to create embankments and walls – such adaptability also reduces the need to cut the tiles. The coloured stripes of the tiles follow an east-to-west orientation and lead the visitor from one area into another. Altogether, it is an ingenious solution with deliberate references to the traditional use of mosaic and tiling in Barcelona's public spaces, and in particular to the work of Antonio Gaudi in Parc Güell.

OPPOSITE Aerial view of the UNESCO Forum 2004 site with the South Eastern Coastal Park in the foreground and the auditorium seating and concert rigging visible. The blue triangular building was designed by Herzog & de Meuron.

ABOVE View of the site and pathways before the planting became fully established. Grasses and trees were selected that are indigenous to natural dunes and could withstand the exposed conditions.

LEFT Building one of the artificial sand dunes, designed to shelter the public from the sea breezes.

LEFT On the boulevard the concrete tiles are used as seats on the left, paving for the street, and as retainers on the embankment wall. The lighting poles are tilted and situated between the benches.

OPPOSITE Views of the distinctive coloured concrete tiles created for this project. They were designed to be strong enough to withstand the weight of trucks passing over them, yet capable of being carried by two workers.

RIGHT and BOTTOM The seating is formed from the artificial dune topography. One auditorium has a capacity of seven thousand and the other two thousand.

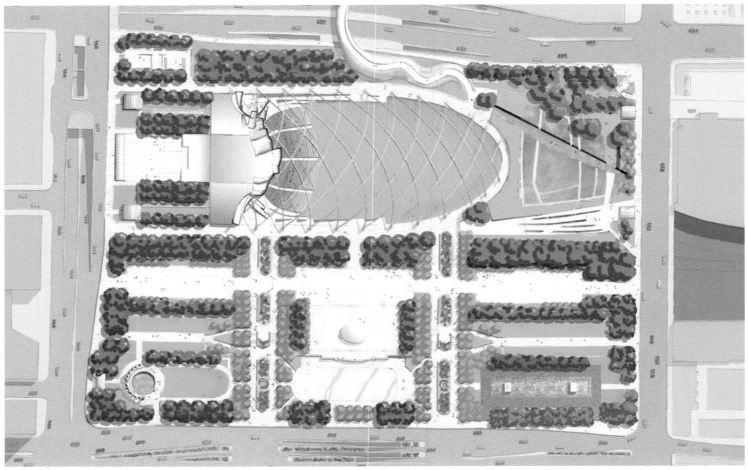

MILLENNIUM PARK
Various designers
Chicago, USA (2005)

This massive 10ha (25 acre) project in Chicago represents an unprecedented combination of architecture, art, and landscape design in a single public space project. The $450 million budget reflects the new value given to the creation of a centrally located park both as an informal recreation space and as a major new events venue. Such an investment endorses the concept of parks as major destinations for cultural activities, both by day and night.

Originally the project's mission was to create new parkland to transform the unsightly railway tracks and car parks that had dotted the lakefront, dating from an era when the city had effectively turned its back on the lake. This simple premise has developed into the most ambitious park project in the US today.

The centrepiece of the park is the Frank Gehry-designed Jay Pritzker Pavilion, a new outdoor concert venue. It consists of a proscenium surrounded by Gehry's trademark curves of stainless steel with a huge steel trellis spanning the entire auditorium. Connected to the pavilion is Gehry's first bridge project, which spans Columbus Drive, linking Millennium Park to the Daley Bicentennial Plaza and Chicago's lakefront park system.

Another major feature is the elliptical jellybean-shaped sculpture by Anish Kapoor, his first public work in the US. To the south-west of the sculpture is the Crown Fountain designed by artist Jaume Plensa. This consists of two 15.24m (50ft) high glass block towers at each end of a shallow reflecting pool. The towers are animated with changing video images and lights, with water cascading down from each one.

Also within the park is the Lurie Garden designed by the team of Kathryn Gustafson, Piet Oudolf, and Robert Israel. This comprises a combination of architecture, planning, and lighting. The garden contains distinct spaces, both large and small, which are defined by sculpted hedgerows and pedestrian pathways. Enclosing the garden on two sides is a 4.5m (15ft) "shoulder" hedge, and a hardwood walkway. This follows a water feature that cuts diagonally through the garden, separating it into a "light plate" with 240 varieties of perennial plants and a "dark plate" shaded by flowering cherry trees. Both by day and night, the Lurie Garden provides a rich and varied sensory experience throughout the seasons.

OPPOSITE (ABOVE) A bird's-eye view of the park, showing Michigan Avenue to the far left and Lake Michigan to the far right. In the foreground are the two monoliths of the Crown Fountain; in the background is the Pritzker Pavillion. The park is framed by Chicago's skyskrapers.

OPPOSITE (BELOW) The plan of the park. The dominant feature is the Jay Pritzker Pavillion, which has fixed seating for 4000 and capacity for an additional 7000 on the lawn. To the right of the pavillion lies the Lurie Garden. Front centre is the Cloudgate Sculpture with the icerink/café terrace in front facing Michigan Avenue.

RIGHT The Cloudgate Sculpture by Annish Kappor. Inspired by liquid mercury, its 110 tons of stainless steel reflects the city's skyline, the clouds, and people passing by on SBC Plaza.

LEFT Detail of the Lurie Garden. The framework in the background is part of the 4.5m (15ft) high shoulder hedge. This represents the description of Chicago as the "city of big shoulders", and the hedge (when fully grown) will enclose the garden on two sides.

BELOW and BOTTOM The Boardwalk in the Lurie Garden is built of Ipe wood and is designed as both a strolling path and a place to gather. The "stream" is bordered by a wide step running the length of the boardwalk; this step is also used for seating so visitors can experience the water more intimately.

ABOVE The Crown Fountain is extremely popular with children, who splash in the shallow pool between two towers which have faces of Chicago citizens projected on LCD screens. Water flows from an outlet located by their mouths, so it appears to spout from them.

LEFT The Jay Pritzker Pavillion, designed by Frank Gehry. The stainless steel ribbons that frame the proscenium stand 36m (120ft) high. They connect to a steel trellis suspended over the lawn seating area. The trellis holds lighting rigs and sound systems.

ABOVE The BP bridge links the Millennium Park with the eastern part of the existing Grant Park and provides views of the city and the lake. It is 282m (925ft) long, has hardwood decking, and is clad in brushed stainless steel panels.

RIGHT Details of the BP Bridge and Lurie Gardens. The bridge has a gentle 5 degree slope to allow easy access for people who are physically challenged. Its sinuous form winds its way over the traffic of Columbus Drive.

LEFT Day and night views of the west side of Lurie Garden. The shoulder hedge is on the right, which protects the more delicate inner garden. The steel grid is a clipping guide, though the hedge will take at least 10 years to mature. The pathway leads to the Pritzker Pavillion.

LEFT and BOTTOM The garden is well illuminated so that it can be enjoyed at night. The garden pays homage to the city's motto *Urbs in horto* (City in a garden), which refers to Chicago's transformation from a marsh into a major city.

LANDFORM UEDA PROJECT

Charles Jencks with Terry Farrell & Partners

Edinburgh, Scotland (2002)

The architects Terry Farrell & Partners were given the responsibilty of masterplanning the area between the Scottish National Gallery of Modern Art and the Dean Gallery in Edinburgh. They commissioned the postmodernist architect, critic, and artist Charles Jencks to create a piece of land art based on his Landform concept, which he had already developed in two works in the extensive gardens of his own home in Dumfries.

The flat and dull former school playing field was transformed into an outdoor sculpture park, with Jencks' Landform Ueda as its centrepiece. The project covers an area of more than 3000 sq m (3588 sq yd) and rises to a height of 7m (23ft). Due to extensive and highly restrictive health and safely measures the final design is a third smaller and less defined than Jencks' original version. Despite these restrictions, it has proved so popular, particularly with children, that the grass has had to be replaced on the most often-used areas.

Careful construction was needed to create the definition of the contours, which the shadows then amplify. The design allows the visitor to walk, sit, slide, and view others. Its design draws inspiration from sources as diverse as neolithic earth works such as the White Horse at Uffington as well as chaos theory and strange attractors, both subjects of great interest to Jencks.

Whatever the references, Landform Ueda works well at many levels: it provides a focus for the lawn space, an aesthetic link between the two galleries, a meeting point, and a destination in its own right.

Jencks comments that, "I envisaged a contemporary version of Seurat's painting *La Grande Jatte*, which depicts people enjoying a sunny afternoon on a grassy riverbank." The project won The Gulbenkian Award for Museum of the Year, which netted the Scottish National Gallery of Modern Art £100,000, equating to a third of the overall cost of the project. It has been highly popular with visitors, too – since its opening visitor numbers to the National Gallery have risen, proving what magnetism such a project can have to an institution.

ABOVE View of the Landform Ueda situated on the former lawn of the Scottish National Gallery of Modern Art. The Landform earthwork also contains three small crescent-shaped ponds. The gallery was formerly the John Watson's Boys School, designed in 1825, and the lawn its playing fields.

LEFT A view showing the *Grand Jatte* effect. The project has proved immediately popular with the public, particularly children. It was the setting for the National Galleries Fun Day in 2003, which attracted over 3,000 children and their families.

LEFT The landform is the final part of a major masterplanning project, linking to the Scottish National Gallery of Modern Art with the Dean Gallery, the new headquarters for the National Galleries of Scotland.

BELOW The grass paths of the project have been designed to accommodate a sit-on lawnmover as the most low-maintenance way of looking after the grass. The project cost £380,000 and took two years to complete.

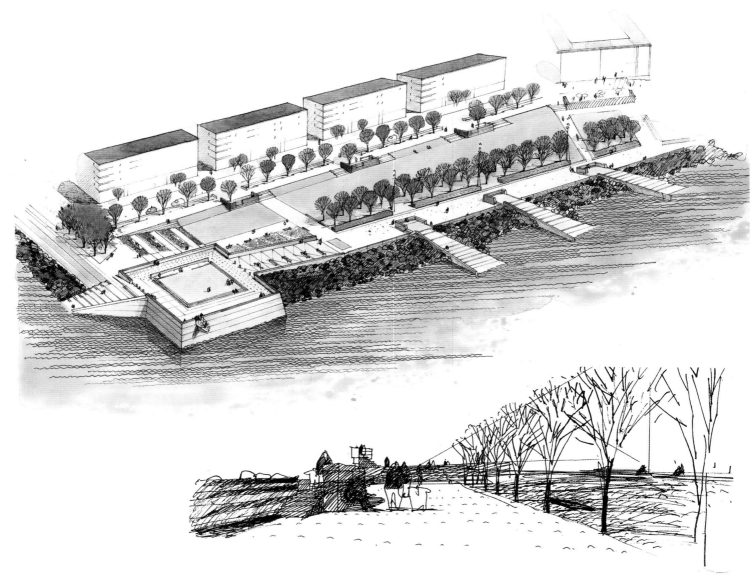

DANIA PARK
Thorbjorn Andersson and PeGe Hillinge SWECO FFNS Architects
Malmö, Sweden (2002)

This park was created from an industrial landfill site which was redeveloped, along with the surrounding new housing and retail area, as part of the west harbour development for the 2001 Expo. The area was desolate and windswept, and because it was the site of a former Saab factory the contaminated soil made it unsuitable for the cultivation of plants and trees.

This proved a tricky challenge for the landscape architect Thorbjorn Andersson, who resolved the problem by making its exposed setting and the big skies and views across the Øresund key features of the design. He created a series of outdoor rooms and viewing points where people could choose whether to be exposed to the elements or sheltered from them, but always remain orientated towards the sea.

The design is very horizontal, working with the flat location and integrating the line of the sky and the horizon into the landscape design. As a landmark project, a generous budget allowed the designers to use superior materials such as granite, larch, and teak to create high-quality elements.

This city park was the first to be created in Malmö for nearly 50 years. It incorporates the Stockholm School tradition of creating open, democratic public spaces full of social activity, where visitors are free to walk on the grass and around the space at their own pace. Despite this tradition, Dania Park is far more architectural in design than its predecessors in the city. Because the design was orientated around constructed spaces, rather than around large areas of planting (that need time to establish themselves), the benefits of the park were evident from the day it opened. It has become incredibly popular and is used regularly as a venue for concerts and even weddings.

Dania Park combines the atmosphere of both the urban city and more rural natural spaces. It displays the expanse and openness of the seaside landscape, yet also incorporates a range of condensed social spaces for different public uses.

ABOVE Perspectives of the site for Dania Park, showing the main elements of the design and the proximity to the new housing that was also developed for the 2001 Expo.

OPPOSITE The Prow is a viewing platform that juts out from the Bastion, and is popular with youths who dive and jump from it – although this wasn't the designer's intention! It is also, rather more surprisingly, a popular backdrop for wedding photographs.

LEFT The Field is an open lawn sheltered by balconies and trees, and the only large public space in the park, with the potential to hold 5000 people. It hosts concerts and festivals and is also popular with sunbathers.

BELOW (TOP) The Prow, a viewing stage popularly used as a diving and jumping platform.

BELOW (BOTTOM) The Bastion is dressed with rough wooden planks that are treated with tar to create a dull black colour. The planks are separated by square pieces of solid stainless steel that shine in the sun. While not approved by the city authorities, the surface has proved irresistible to the local youths who love to climb on it.

ABOVE and LEFT
The Balconies, three open wooden boxes in larch which are furnished with teak benches. They are sheathed with shingles stained black with tar, providing a visual and aural reference to boats. The Balconies are set into the short slope that overlooks a grass meadow known as The Field. Two of them are reached by steps and the third by a slope, also accessible by wheelchair. Each balcony can hold 15 people.

LEFT Detail from inside one of the balconies that overlooks The Field, which is set below ground level to give additional protection from the wind.

BELOW View into one of the Scouts; three tiled concrete slipways that lead down to the sea and are popular for sunbathing. The rear wall is soiid granite, contains bench seating, and acts as a windbreak, as do the concrete walls that separate each Scout. The light sources were designed to be unobtrusive.

OPPOSITE The boundary that separates the park from an area destined for future housing development. The trees *Sorbus latifolia* are both salt- and wind-resistant. The low wall provides additional seating for events, and the high-quality and simple palette of materials and finishes are well detailed and maintained.

ANCHOR PARK
SLA Landscape Architects
Vastra Hamnen, Malmö, Sweden (2001)

Anchor Park is a canal-side project in Vastra Hamnen, a new residential area of Malmö in southern Sweden, designed by the Danish landscape architect Stig Andersson of SLA. The site was formerly a harbour, a run-down area that was developed for the 2001 Housing Expo.

The most dramatic feature of the scheme is the biomorphic canal-bank walkway, constructed from high-quality concrete cast in situ, which undulates for over 1km (¾ mile) alongside the canal. It is a graphic design, the white concrete contrasting with alternating layers of seven different grasses that form a composition of varying tones and. Along with the oak, willow, and beech groves, these make up the majority of the park.

It is a new type of urban park that has been developed according to ecological considerations. The groves require very little maintenance – in fact, any intervention required here is contrary to the intentions of the architect. These zones give the park its unique character.

Andersson wanted the space to be "a celebration of change as a basic condition of life and a collection of elements that constantly morph from one state to another". One of his "vessels for change" is the use of impressed circle motifs on the surface of the concrete that are designed, after rain, to transform into puddles that reflect the sky, helping to create an ever-changing surface. Large Swedish boulders have also been laid in the concrete.

Maintenance is always a major issue for any public space project. Anchor Park has been designed to actually accommodate some natural decay in terms of the concrete slabs, the 20 tonnes of pebbles in the water that are expected to be covered by seaweed, and the growth of grasses that will survive without much maintenance. Andersson states that, "various materials have been set into play with one another, now one just has to wait and see what happens – as landscape architecture becomes nature."

OPPOSITE An aerial view of the park showing its main features: the concrete boardwalk, the defined areas of planting, the bug-like footbridges, and scattered concrete seating. Each element has an organic shape, and the spaces flow into each other.

LEFT Detail of the concrete boardwalk with an insert wooden deck just seen to the right. The rubber footbridge leads nowhere, but allows visitors to step out over the canal. Tonnes of pebbles were added to the water.

BELOW Plan of the park, showing that while the western shore of the canal is a straight line running in front of the new residential buildings, the eastern shore of Anchor winds along following a more organic design.

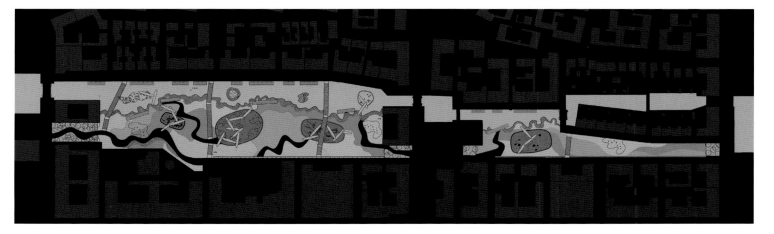

ABOVE Groves of oak, beech, and willow trees surrounded by free-growing grasses have created a naturalistic and low-maintenance environment.

ABOVE A string of fibre-optics traces the line where the water and the bank meet, casting a glimmer of light across the surface of the water and creating an artificial phosphorescence. It also acts as a safety feature at night in the absence of railings.

ABOVE and RIGHT The park's design becomes even more graphic in winter when covered with snow. Conventional seating approaches were all rejected and replaced by 137 rocks and a number of concrete stumps spread across the space.

BELOW The variety of materials makes walking or lingering in Anchor Park a sensual experience. Wooden panels, rocks, patterns in glass and concrete, and stools are set into the concrete path. The bridge leads over the canal to the housing beyond.

COLUMBINE GARDEN
SLA Landscape Architects
Copenhagen, Denmark (2001)

The Columbine Garden (so named after the white-clad sweetheart of Pierrot) is a small 500 sq m (600 sq yd) project that has created a new flower garden in the Tivoli Gardens, Copenhagen. This mid-19th-century 8ha (20 acre) park is situated in the heart of the city and is a mix of flower gardens, cafés, a concert hall, and amusements including a Ferris wheel. The Tivoli Gardens has continued the tradition of floral planting since its creation – in a single year more than 135,000 new bulbs are planted.

This little flower garden provides a graphic and contemporary addition to the formal and traditional planting within the main park. The Columbine Garden is spatially defined by the dark-green yew hedges that surround the organically curving flowerbeds.

Four different varieties of fragrant white flowers are planted during Tivoli's annual season, which lasts for five months, and the plants chosen vary in growth and shape to add variety. They are densely planted in the tradition of carpet bedding but are not traditional low-lying bedding-plant varieties. The Columbine Garden was planted with 4000 cream-coloured daffodils for the Tivoli's season opening in 2001, followed by 1200 dahlias in the summer, and then, to end the season, 600 white Japanese anemones. The Tivoli employs an army of gardeners to maintain the many gardens.

The design of the beds and paths is organic and curvaceous. The paths are constructed in a bright-red brown rubber that muffles and cushions the sound of footsteps; this means that the visitor walks silently through the garden, adding to the feeling of quiet contemplation. This part of the garden contrasts with the crunchy gravel paths found in the rest of the park.

The translucent polycarbonate cylinders dotted throughout the garden illuminate the beds and emit slow and varying rhythms of bright-white to muted warm-yellow light. The Tivoli stays open until midnight during the week and 1 am.

LEFT and BELOW Two views of Riley-Levin Children's Garden at Swindler Cove Park. The garden features 18 large planting beds, where children tend flowers and edible plants, a berry garden, a butterfly garden, and a herb garden where they experience different textures and scents. It serves hundreds of economically disadvantaged children from the Washington Heights and Inwood communities of Upper Manhatten. Topics such as recycling, responsible use of water, and organic gardening are discussed and children learn the basic principles of nutrition.

SWINDLER COVE PARK
New York Restoration Project (NYRP)
New York, USA (2003)

The actress Bette Midler founded the New York Restoration Project in 1995 in the belief that clean neighbourhoods and green city spaces are fundamental to the quality of life of each citizen. During an interview with *Good Housekeeping* magazine, Midler said, "When I moved to New York I was very disappointed at how parts of the city looked … People were throwing their garbage out the window, leaving their lunches on the ground. Finally, I realized I actually needed to do something – even if I had to pick up the stuff with my own two hands."

Modelled on the Central Park Conservancy, the NYRP liaises with individual residents, community-based groups, and public agencies to reclaim, restore, and develop under-resourced parks, community gardens, and open spaces in New York City. It primarily targets economically disadvantaged neighbourhoods where illegal dumping, litter, graffiti, and vandalism have become all-too-familiar sights in parks and open spaces that are not regularly maintained.

In just under a decade, NYRP has accomplished a great deal. It has removed over 80,000 tonnes of garbage from project sites, reclaimed more than 162ha (400 acres) of under-resourced and abandoned parkland along the banks of the Hudson and Harlem rivers, and rescued scores of community gardens from commercial development.

Swindler Cove Park is an entirely new, 2ha (5 acre) park created in northern Manhattan on the site of what was once an illegal dumping ground on the Harlem River.

It was opened to the public in August 2003 and represents the full spectrum of NYRP's efforts to reclaim open space for the benefit of under-served communities. Between 1996 and 1999, NYRP removed thousands of tonnes of garbage, construction debris, and sunken boats from this waterfront site to transform the reclaimed land into a magnificent riverfront park. Swindler Cove Park now features restored wetlands, native plantings, a freshwater pond, and pathways. The park is also home to the Riley-Levin Children's Garden and the Peter Jay Sharp Boathouse.

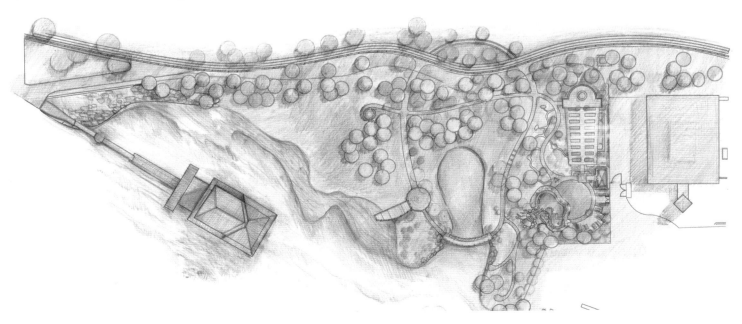

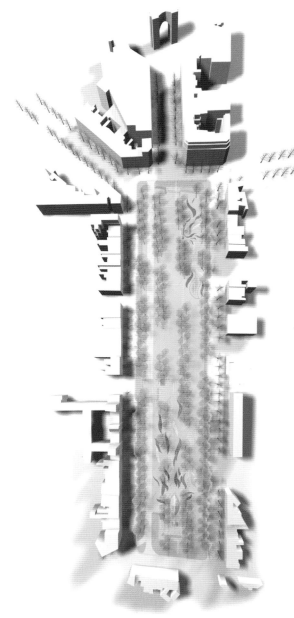

ABOVE Seating is designed as an integral part of the perimeter fencing with wooden slates added to the curving metal backrests. West 8 wanted the fencing to be painted black, but the city of Lille preferred a more vibrant red, a colour that does dominate rather too much.

ABOVE RIGHT Plan of the transformed boulevard, showing its connections with nearby traffic lanes: it occupies a position in a residential area surrounded by apartment blocks and cafés. The fencing has been designed at such a scale that it creates its own monumental "block".

PARK J B LEBAS
West 8 Landscape Architects
Lille, France (2005)

The aim of this project was to transform the historic Boulevard J B Lebas into an urban park, removing the former roads and parking, and directing traffic around the perimeter of the park. The plan was to create a project in the style of an 18th-century public space, but also to include strong contemporary influences.

The original boulevard had a monumental row of chestnut trees running along its length toward the Ponte de Paris, the historic gateway at the top of the park. Some of these trees had been damaged by parking bays and other constructions, so the avenue of trees has been fully restored.

The most striking aspect of the park is its perimeter fencing, which is 4m (13ft) high and painted red. This dominating element has a variety of elements integrated within it, including large gates and information panels; however, the most interesting component is the seating, which allows the visitor to sit half in or out of the park.

There are three sections to the park, the first consisting of dense flowerbeds and a children's play area that includes a small hillock. The second section, still to be completed, will have pavilion terraces and a *jeu de boules*. The third section, also still at the planning stage, will consist of an interactive water sculpture. The idea is for this to take people by surprise and, by enabling them to direct the angle of the water flow, make them more emotionally involved in the park.

What is most remarkable about the design is that the arrangement and the major elements are essentially traditional ones – a pavilion, formal flower beds, a fountain, and a water sculpture – but all of them have been given a contemporary twist. It is no coincidence that Adriaan Geuze of West 8 is a keen devotée of traditional parks, and names the Vondels Park in Amsterdam and Hyde Park in London as two of his favourite public spaces.

Bizarrely, the local bus company has insisted on including a bus line that runs through the park. The impact of this has yet to become apparent.

ABOVE and LEFT View from outside the park. The curves created by the seating elements in the fencing have been replicated as a motif, both concave and convex, around the park to break up the monotony of the fencing.

ABOVE and RIGHT The flowerbeds have been designed along traditional 19th-century principles of carpet bedding that provides vivid and intense splashes of colour. The essential difference, however, is that their crescent-moon-shaped beds spill out from the formal lawns onto the paving as if trying to escape.

LEFT Additional 20m (22yd) benches have been added within the park. They come from the same family as those, also designed by West 8, produced for the Schouwburg Plaza in Rotterdam.

OPPOSITE With its high fencing and limited access points, the park is popular with both children and parents who can clearly see their children along the straight pathways – this also allows the children some freedom to explore on their own.

"The place we are gathered right now is also a world summit in its own right … as we stand here on Somoho I want to remind delegates that this shows what you can do without waiting for governments to tell you what to do. Wherever I go I shall always treasure my memory of this encounter on the inspirational Soweto Mountain of Hope."

Kofi Annan

NEW USES FOR OLD SPACES

THE DECLINE OF MANUFACTURING, heavy industries, power stations, dockyards, and rail freight in our cities has created opportunities to transform these derelict areas into new public spaces, many of which on a far larger scale than traditional public spaces. Rubbish dumps and contaminated wastes sites are another area of potential redevelopment, as are highways and reservations as the dominance of cars and the huge traffic highways that carved up our cites from the 1960s onwards are re-evaluated and scaled down.

As people move back into our cities and choose to use them for recreation instead of leaving them to play, cities have literally cleaned up areas that were former dumping grounds. This regeneration has public space creation at its heart, going hand in hand with the conversion of former warehouses, factories and commercial properties into housing and workspaces ensuring a 24-hour community. The waterfronts that were devoted to commerce have been transformed into leisure areas, giving back to the public access to their rivers and harbours.

The transformation often has been accompanied with an examination and preservation of some elements of the previous use – a reminder of local heritage and the massive changes our cites are undergoing.

The Westergasfabriekpark in Amsterdam is a former gasworks which has retained many of its original buildings on the site, converting them into work space for creative and media businesses. This new park is situated in a residential district of the city and next to a traditional park. Its design and function is more as a thriving series of arts venues, school, café, and lido – with its huge ribbon pool for children to splash in and a nature area for exploring, which complements well the formal design of the existing park it borders.

The history of the site is well documented, and the massive gasholders remain either as foundations transformed into lily ponds or as a gigantic venue for temporary events. The mix of events and workspaces keeps the park animated at all times, so that it is a vibrant and related part of the community that surrounds it.

The project manger Evert Verhagen admits that the creation and opening of such a project is only the beginning, as it takes time for such projects to find their direction and he is constantly surprised at the way the public chooses to use them. Therefore the design must be flexible enough to adapt to changing patterns and uses. If spaces are too rigidly programmed with a preconceived notion of how they will be used it can often turn out to be wrong. Local communities who may be the biggest user group may have very specific needs and new requirements can be identified with careful study of the way the public choose to utilize these new types of public spaces. Spaces on this scale offer the possibility for experimentation and trying different approaches and should continue developing and changing so that they,

PREVIOUS PAGE An abandoned shopping trolley can be transformed into an attractive oversize planter. This is part of Eco Design student Clare Cunningham's "Re-enchanting The City" project, looking at how to bring back beauty and connectivity to the urban environment.

OPPOSITE The foundations of two gasholders in the Westergasfabriek park in Amsterdam have lent their form well to a transformation into two interconnecting ponds, complete with waterfowl and reeds.

unlike many traditional parks of the past, do not find themselves under-utilized and forgotten. Evert feels the fewer design rules there are when a project such as this is undertaken the better the results. The designer Kathryn Gustafsen describes the first four years of a new project such as Westergasfabriek as "crucial", since it takes that long for vegetation to take hold and for all parties to understand how the space will work.

The Zhongshan Shipyard park in China also celebrates and acknowledges the heritage of its site, transforming many of the former industrial structures as backdrops to the landscape design. Like Westergasfabriek, it adds new design elements so that it doesn't feel like a museum site. The design leads you around the various elements of the park, but also allows plenty of opportunities to explore, clamber, and make your own discoveries in a way it would be hard to find in the more litigious West. The designers aimed to create a project that has specificity, and were determined to use only native plants despite opposition from the local authorities, who are still looking to the West for inspiration in landscape design.

The Westblak Skatepark project in Rotterdam is a clever way to create a

new amenity in the city centre without the need for any major upheaval. A central reservation, one of the most wasteful types of the many dismal spaces postwar traffic planning has created (J G Ballard's novel *Concrete Island* explores these hidden spaces and a possible fascinating scenario), has been converted into a park for skate boarders, a user group whom are usually given far more peripheral spaces. The reservation, surrounded by high fencing, provides a place to meet

for not only skateboarders but pedestrians travelling the length of this long and dull road, keeping them away from the traffic and offering them points of rest.

The A13 Arterial project also looks at similar traffic-dominated spaces. Its aims are rather different, however: to try to appeal to both local residents and commuting motorists by creating a series of links and landmarks along an unremarkable stretch of highway in order to give it a sense of place and to

ABOVE A boarder enjoying Westblaak Skatepark in Rotterdam, which was created from a traffic central reservation. This user group's needs are rarely catered for, leaving them to appropriate other public spaces not designed for them, often to the annoyance of others.

OPPOSITE At Westblaak skate park, in addition to providing a variety of special equipment for skaters, a building was created on the site which will be function as a cafe and meeting point for the general public who also use the space to watch the boarders in action.

create better spaces for the local community to pass through going about their daily lives. The lead architect, Tom de Paor, describes it as "a strategy for the margins and edges of the A13 trunk road corridor: to choreograph serial and individual objects in space ... the vehicle windscreen performs as a moving proscenium within which the changing composition is constantly framed. Arterial is a journey through interlinking, imaginative landscape on a grand scale, with ideas, theme, and connections set up to fire your curiosity and make a whole new road experience."

The project created design and artworks from familiar roadway elements. These include high-security link fencing given a coating of white reflective paint in order to create a ripple effect, central reservation lighting which is also an installation, and grass verges which become land art – imaginative ways to improve our most urban and visually depressing public environment.

Due to its extremely ambitious programme, not all of the planned elements were completed. However, the project has encouraged the local borough to actively ensure that high-quality art and design is included in its public places, routes and housing developments and has injected energy into area that sorely needed it.

Somoho – Soweto Mountain of Hope – is a story of a community reclaiming a seriously dangerous no-go area (a piece of wasteland with a water tower at the centre) and creating a focus for community activities and action. The design content has been subtle,

consisting of the basic transformation of a former water tower into a community centre and beacon for gatherings, but this helped to create a better community project, utilizing the local materials and manpower available. The project has also brought out the design creativity of the community itself, and community ownership is felt in every element of the project. The reused tower gave a focus to the project, which continues to grow and spread around its base.

The Nature Playground in Copenhagen, Demark took an old rubbish dumping area actually situated within a park (the Valbyparken) and created a new nature playground for children. Here, the designer Helle Nebelong tackled the resulting problem of what to do with unsuitable earth containing rubbish from the dump by using it to build a series of small hills which separate the playground from the remainder fo the park. One of the key points here is the concept of designing a playground that doesn't exclude adults and moves away from the cliché that playgrounds should be full of bright colours, standardized equipment and smiling, overgrown toys. As Nebelong says, "it is so often quite simple things which awaken a child's curiosity. If everything is not the same and predictable a child's fantasy is sharpened, and if the challenges are there he will practice climbing up into complicated twisted trees, throwing small stones at targets and jumping from one big stone to another".

According to Nebelong it is the commissioners of playgrounds who ask

OPPOSITE A former shipyard in Zhongshan, China, has become a major new landmark, park, and tourist attraction for the city. Many of the original industrial structures have been kept, but transformed to create striking sculptural features.

for bright colours, not the children. She sees the increasing standardization of playgrounds as dangerous because play becomes simplified and the child doesn't have to worry or take care about his movements – he doesn't have to estimate distance, height, and risk, which requires developing skills that are necessary for life outside such safe environments.

It would be possible to create an entire book of new public spaces that have transformed spaces with former industrial, waste, or commercial use of some kind. These spaces are all around us in some form, and can result in some of the most dramatic transformation in public space design.

WESTBLAAK SKATEPARK CONCEPT

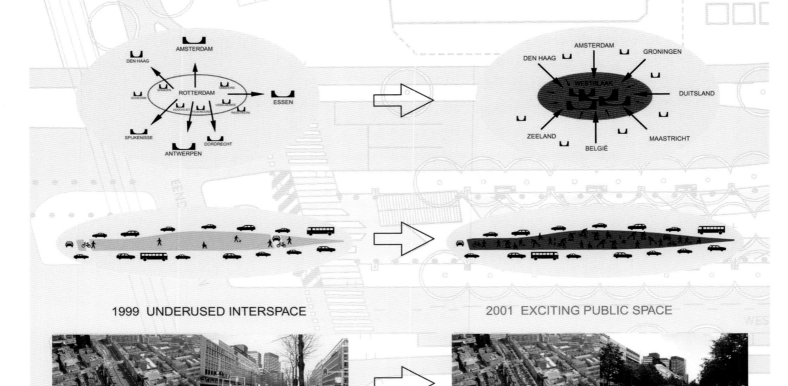

1999 UNDERUSED INTERSPACE

2001 EXCITING PUBLIC SPACE

dS+V
Gemeente Rotterdam

WESTBLAAK SKATEPARK
dS+V Urban Planning Services
Rotterdam, The Netherlands (2005)

This new skatepark was created from the entire elongated central reservation of the Westblaak Road. It is the largest and most comprehensive outdoor skatepark in the Netherlands. Its popularity with skaters is partly because of its exceptional size and partly because of its location in the centre of the city.

Besides skaters, the park is also attractive to inhabitants and employees from the neighbourhood, who rest on the numerous benches to watch the skaters. The benches have been designed with a steel strip making them suitable as skating objects too.

The most striking elements of the skatepark are the 11 pieces of specially created equipment. The large half-pipe, the mini-ramp, and the elaborated course meet the requirements of an extremely varied skating public. Skateboarders, in-line skaters, BMX riders, and rollerskaters can all find something here, and there are challenges not only for professional skaters but also for beginners. The stainless steel equipment was specially designed and manufactured for this location to allow spectacular stunts can be performed. To achieve this, it was of vital importance that skaters were continuously and intensively involved in the design process.

This is an excellent example of an imaginative project that has reclaimed a previously dead space. Such projects create new destinations and improve the area visually, as well as helping to reduce crime by their activity. It proves too that even a central reservation can have a new life of its own.

The project is so successful that the city organizes small and large events in the park all year long and the project won an honourable mention in the second European Prize for Urban Public Space.

The skatepark was designed by Dirk van Peijpe of dS+V in Rotterdam, a firm that provide urban planning services. The cabin was designed by BAR architects, the skate objects by Solos International, and the graphic design for the painted asphalt pavement was created by 75B.

OPPOSITE Before and after. Skating facilities often end up on the periphery of a city in neglected or soulless spaces and are purely aimed at those involved in the sport rather than providing interest to other users. Its scale and central location is why this skatepark has become an attractive venue for skaters from the whole country.

RIGHT The asphalt surface has been painted red, blue, black, and white. The coloured surfaces emphasize the function of the central reservation as a skatepark, and a circulation space for passers-by has been incorporated into the colour pattern. The plan is to refresh the paintwork every couple of years – this kind of active maintainance and management schedule is vital to stop such spaces becoming shabby and unattractive.

ABOVE A metal cabin in the skatepark provides modest accommodation for the staff and also contains public toilets. The staff, present every day, supervise the site, provide first aid, and report any soiling. Graffiti is removed immediately.

LEFT View from the pavement across the traffic to the central reservation. The whole space has been fringed with large Linden trees.

LEFT Behind the stainless steel skating ramps a small building has been constructed from gabions (rock-filled steel cages) and will become a café. A pavement café is also planned.

RIGHT A laurel hedge (which is planned to grow to a height of 1.5m/5ft) separates the skatepark from the adjacent roadways. When fully grown, the hedge will act as a visual, acoustic, and additional safety barrier. Thanks to simple lampposts on the edge of the reservation, the park can also be used in the evening.

ABOVE Bird's-eye view of the park separated from the residential neighbourhood by a canal to the south and rail tracks to the north. Two of the former gas tanks have been dismantled and converted into lakes. The main cluster of buildings referred to as "The Village" is located in the bottom right-hand corner of the site.

RIGHT The hard landscaping area which surrounds the original buildings – converted into workshops and studios for creative industries – provides an excellent event space. Behind it is the canal, which separates Westergasfabriek from the local residential area. A new bridge has been added to provide access.

WESTERGASFABRIEK CULTURE PARK
Gustafson Porter Landscape Architects
Amsterdam, The Netherlands (2005)

This project involved the transformation of a former gasworks into a new cultural park in a residential district of Amsterdam. The buildings on the site had already been used as cultural venues since the closure of the gasworks in 1967, but this had been seen as an interim usage until a permanent function could be found. The 20 ha (50 acre) site contains 19 buildings, including a large, round gas tank, which is now a major temporary events space.

Many of the earlier buildings (dating from 1885) are protected and were restored and have been let to creative companies. Other buildings include cafés, a nursery, and event spaces.

The competition for the project was won by Kathryn Gustafson on behalf of her company Gustafson Porter Landscape Architects. Her design changes in character from an eastern to a western emphasis, ranging from a formal urban park to a looser design with more scope for nature, with wilder planting, and meandering pathways for visitors to exlpore. Although contemporary in its overall design, the project has a number of traditional elements, such as a large green field, ponds, and intersecting paths. Evert Verhagen, the project manager at Westergasfabriek since 1990, describes the project as "one big roof garden" because the soil on the site was so contaminated that the landscaping project had to be built on a layer of new soil added over the capped ground and water system.

One of the most expensive elements of the park is the use of reinforced grass, which is so robust that it eliminates unsightly bald patches. The soil in Amsterdam is very peaty, and the grass does not wear well under heavy use; therefore the reinforced grass has turned out to be an excellent investment. Evert Verhagen says, "The park is a living thing, constantly developing and changing, and you have to view it that way – some things don't work and then you have to explore other approaches. We are still learning about how people will use the park. We haven't informed the way the places are used, but have created robust and flexible spaces and an environment that encourages people to think and rethink. The only plan for the events programme is to try to attract different kinds of audiences for events who may not be conventional park users."

ABOVE Kathyrn Gusafson's winning design, entitled "Changement", was produced in collaboration with Francine Houben of Mecanoo. The proposal was a park that promises different experiences through the changing seasons; the completed project is very close to her original design.

BELOW The events field, where the shallow geometric ribbon pool forms the northern boundary of the field. The bottom of the pool is covered in black concrete and natural stone, which reflects the broad Dutch skyscape.

RIGHT In the water garden at the western end of the park an artificial stream carries water over several waterfalls. The stream and path alongside it are crossed by two bridges, but adults and children are happy to remove their footwear and walk across the waterfall.

ABOVE One of the more intimate spaces created, which runs along the northern side of the park. the path allows the visitor to wander by the side of the stream. The bridge takes pedestrians and cyclists into the Cité des Artistes (a series of workshops for fashion designers and other creatives) at the end of the park.

LEFT Tracks for joggers and cyclists have been incorporated into the design. The sloping bank to the left provides a physical and acoustic barrier to the rail tracks beyond.

LEFT The North Plaza, covered with yellow gravel, is where the new Westergasfabriek meets the old park. It is also the start of the ribbon pool.

BELOW LEFT The Reed Garden. The reeds act as a natural filter.

BOTTOM Panorama of the wet gardens, including the reed garden centre right and the low waterfall in the foreground. The management and containment of water refers to the Netherlands' tradition of polders, dykes, and land reclamation.

LEFT At Charlton Crescent Subway artist Anu Patel redesigned the landscape on both sides of the subway, painted the interior, and added sequenced LED lighting bands positioned at regular intervals along the circular bore of the funnel.

BELOW and BOTTOM Twin Roundabouts by Thomas Heatherwick Studio treats each roundabout as part of the road, deforming the tarmac skin into a peaked conical form fabricated from sprayed concrete on a steel mesh attached to steel cables. The height of each roundabout corresponds directly to their width, with each structure's vertical curve being the same as its horizontal radius. A pedestrian crossing that runs across the roundabout also means that the experience is not limited to vehicular traffic.

ARTERIAL A13 ARTSCAPE PROJECT
Tom de Paor and Others
Barking and Dagenham, London (2004)

The Arterial A13 Artscape Project is one of the largest and most ambitious public arts projects in the UK. Its aim was to improve the environment of the A13, a major highway in Barking and Dagenham, by introducing artist-designed landscapes, greener verges, cycleways and footpaths, lighting schemes, refurbished subways, and landmark features to punctuate the route and signify a sense of place.

The project originated in 1997 as a partnership between the London Borough of Barking and Dagenham and Transport for London. Architect Tom de Paor was commissioned as the lead artist/designer, and it was he who came up with the Arterial concept.

The project involved extensive public consultations and community involvement. Tom de Paor describes the concept as a "strategy for the margins and edges of the A13 trunk-road corridor, to choreograph serial and individual objects in space and produce a unified temporal experience … The vehicle windscreen acts as a moving proscenium within which the changing composition is constantly framed. Arterial is a journey through interlinking imaginative landscape on a grand scale, with ideas, themes and connections set up to fire your curiosity and make a whole new road experience."

The individual pieces on the A13 that make up the project are located on and off the roadside: junctions, round-abouts, subways, and community areas affected by the road, including parks and local housing estates. Individual projects range from the refurbishment of dark and neglected subways, new landscaping to create privacy from the road for residents and pedestrians and new green areas for the public, lighting and sculptural installations, new public seating, and playgrounds.

The roll-call of designers and artists involved includes Thomas Heatherwick, MUF Architecture Art, Kinnear Landscape Architects, Graham Ellard, and Stephen Johnstone. The project was a victim of its (perhaps) overambitious programme and local antisocial behaviour, but is a brave attempt to tackle urban blight. The projects have benefited the local community directly in terms of facilities, but have also given them, and those driving past, a recognizable sense of identity.

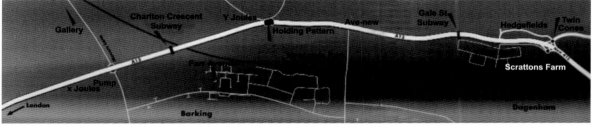

RIGHT A map showing the section of the A13 road which features these projects – ranging from art installations to revamped subways and parks.

ABOVE "Landing Pattern" is a light work clustered beneath the flyover of the A13 motorway. It was designed by Graham Ellara and Stephen Johnstone in collaboration with Tom de Paor. The work consists of 74 stainless steel needles 5.5m (18ft) high, their tips formed by blue airport taxi way lights.

RIGHT and BOTTOM The location of each needle is organized according to the geometry of the nearby roads. The title of the design reflects its position beneath a flyover and flight path.

RIGHT Farr Avenue, a small shopping precinct on Thames View Estate, was cut off from the rest of the borough by the A13, with poor facilities for residents. As part of "Diversion", a spinoff from the Arterial A13 Project, Jason Cornish and Phil Power designed a new hard landscaping scheme that incorporates paving, granite seating which expands or recedes depending on your perspective, lighting, and tree planting. The scheme has encouraged residents to use this space as a place to sit and relax.

RIGHT This pump designed by Tom de Paor and lighting artist Clare Brew contains the electrical control system for the bypass's drainage system. It is constructed from high-quality precast white concrete panels polished and protected with an anti-graffiti coating. The Led lights are sequenced to create different repeated patterns.

NATURE PLAYGROUND

Helle Nebelong Landscape Architect

Valbyparken, Copenhagen, Denmark (2005)

Valbyparken is the largest park in Copenhagen and has been totally renovated over the last eight years.

For the last four years a 20,000 sq m (23,920 sq yd) playground has been under construction using manual labour from an unemployment project. The area had formerly been used as a rubbish dump, so the old contaminated earth had to be cleared away into hillocks and a new layer of clean soil added.

Helle Nebelong (a landscape architect who works partly for the municipality of Copenhagen and partly for her own private practice, Sansehaver) designed a plan consisting of various organic elements: a large area with sand and gravel, small green islands, winding paths, a village of woven willow huts and fences, a wild-flower area, and a snail-shaped mound with a path spiralling up to a lookout point. The whole playground design is pulled together by a circular 210m (230 yd) long wooden bridge or boardwalk.

Helle is also president of the Danish Playground Association, and has designed the playground to allow children to explore by themselves. As Helle says, " It is important that children be allowed to find out the nature of things by themselves, everything should not be explained and demystified beforehand."

One of the most striking aspects of the playground is the lack of bright colours, smiley faces, and overgrown toys in the design. The space could just as easily be enjoyed by adults wandering through as by children, and does not exclude adults physically or aesthetically. Helle believes "It is a mistaken adult idea that everything to do with children must be openly amusing and painted in bright colours. A child's day is already full to bursting with colours and moving images from the colourful interior of the day-care centre, to hours in front of a TV or computer. Children need to be able to relax their eyes and their minds when they come outside. Nature's own colours are perfect for a playground."

This approach means that though the development is primarily a playground, it still appears part of, rather than separate from the rest of the Valbyparken.

LEFT A plan of the park showing the circular wooden bridge and snail-shaped lookout mound to the bottom right.

BELOW Five towers were situated at intervals along the bridge, each with a different theme. On the far left is the Green Tower, which is built around an existing tree, and on the far right the Wind Tower, whose crooked appearance is designed to appear windblown.

OPPOSITE LEFT A landscape created with boulders and with new planting still growing in. The design encourages children to clamber, explore, and make decisions about risking jumping and so on, rather than relying on rubber matting to break their fall.

OPPOSITE RIGHT Willow fences and huts provide shelters and secret spaces for children to hide, play and develop their imagination. This is very different from the usual playground approach of clear sightlines and exposed elements.

OPPOSITE BOTTOM Product and furniture students from Denmark's Design School worked with Helle Nebelong to create the towers. In the background can be seen the light tower which has stained glass panels designed to be viewed from inside the structure.

LEFT Local craftsman Henrick Andersen carved these climbing bears from existing tree stumps.

BELOW The wooden decking was constructed from local trees destroyed by Dutch Elm disease. The area is supervised on weekdays, but at weekends families are free to enjoy it as they wish.

ABOVE Children play in a dugout canoe on a sand and gravel "river". Areas like this help to stimulate children's imaginations.

ABOVE The site for the Somoho Mountain of Hope, with the water tower surrounded by typical "matchbox" homes, with squatter homes on the far right. The wasteland had previously segregated different racial groups and had formed a boundary of the community, rather than, as now, being the focus of it.

RIGHT The wasteland was so dangerous that people would walk the long way around the perimeter to visit friends, rather than risk being mugged or raped by taking the short cut across it.

SOMOHO MOUNTAIN OF HOPE
Katy Marks & Amandla Waste Creations
Soweto, South Africa (2002)

The Johannesburg Parks Authority felled the majority of trees on this notorious waste-land site in Soweto in an effort to stop muggers jumping down from the trees and attacking the public. It was this drastic action, which did nothing to tackle the root cause of the problem, that prompted the local community to create the Somoho Mountain of Hope project.

During the Apartheid era Amandla Mentoor, a community leader, organized groups of youths to collect waste in Soweto; this was then used to create papier-mâché art. This project became known as Amandla Waste Creations. The fact that the group had outgrown their original space was the driving force behind the plan to transform the "mountain" to act as a community centre for their work.

British architect Katy Marks came up with simple, low-cost ways to transform the tower into a usable building. The metal-working skills needed for fabrication of the new staircase and grille, and the painting labour, were sourced from the local community by Amandla. Having started with just five volunteers the project eventually had 200 people working on its development.

The tower is now used for community workshops, dance and weaving classes and a wooden stage has been built at the base for larger-scale events. The project is constantly evolving, and has opened up discussions about the use of buildings and the types of amenities needed within the community. The wasteland has been transformed from a dangerous place to a buzzing, colourful hub for learning, creativity, and imagination.

One local resident, Hilda Nekhumbe, said, "The mountain was scary. I never ever thought that I would sit here, and I am really surprised – things do happen. You can see it was a dangerous place: I used to attend school on the other side but instead of walking across I would always take the long route. They used to rape and mug people. Now it is clean and the gardens are beautiful, everyone wants to be here and can relax and not be afraid. Even little kids can play here, something I never dreamed of. It has given hope to the community."

TOP LEFT Metal grilles were created from industrial off-cuts and bike parts to create safety barriers. The colour scheme was loosely based on the South African flag, but the final design was structured by the paint colours that could be bought most cheaply.

TOP RIGHT The staircase was added to provide better access to the floors of the tower than the ladder that had been there previously. The rails were constructed from former Royal Mail delivery bicycles: these had been shipped over from the UK for the community's use, and when worn out were recycled to become part of the railings.

LEFT Crowds gather on the day that Kofi Annan visited the project during the World Summit in September 2002. The event was packed with children who would have formerly been too scared to visit the space.

BELOW The first priority for the community was to announce their intention to reclaim the space and outline their vision for the project. The papier-mâché figure is holding the world in his hands, symbolizing the fact that youth represents the future.

Zhongshan Shipyard Park
Turenscape & the Centre for Landscape Architecture at Beijing University
Zhongshan, China (2002)

This new park was created on the site of a former shipyard in the city of Zhongshan in the province of Guangdong in southern China. It had very clear objectives, firstly to improve the landscape of the city's downtown area in which it was located. It was also intended to create new recreational opportunities for local people, to become a site for environmental and historical education, and to develop as a tourist attraction.

The designers were keen to ensure that the new park became an integral part of the urban fabric of the city rather than being isolated from it, and that the cultural changes in China that had led to the demise of the shipyard should be seen as a significant part of the city's recent history. This they combined with a philosophy that "weeds can be just as beautiful as roses".

The park was the first to be created in China where the

location had an industrial heritage – the shipyard was built in the 1950s and went bankrupt in 1999. Although small in scale, covering an area of 11ha (27 acres), the project reflects 50 years of socialist history in China.

The undeveloped site contained a lake, a wide variety of existing trees and vegetation, and the wreckage of docks, cranes, rail-tracks, and water towers. The lake is connected through the River Qijiang to the sea, with water levels fluctuating here up to 1m (3ft) daily. To solve this issue, a network of bridges was constructed at various levels and integrated with terraced planting to keep visitors above the waterline.

The rusting industrial elements from the shipyard were treated in various ways: some were preserved and restored, others were modified, and some were removed and new forms created in their place. The principal designer, Professor Kongjian Yu, who founded Turenscape (whose philosophy is "nature, man and spirits as one") was keen to avoid an out-of-context design that mimicked early 20th-century European or American landscaping. Instead, he embraced one that respected the history and cultural identity of this industrial, Asian landscape.

TOP A former crane creates a gateway at the western entrance to the park. In the distance, two bronze figures of ship-workers can be seen – these have become a popular location for photographs.

ABOVE LEFT and RIGHT One new design feature is a sculptural grid of 180 white columns that are illuminated at night. On the right is an avenue of bamboo trees where shadow boxing is often practised.

LEFT The former dock sheds were stripped to their bare bones and then painted and transformed into tea houses and a club house. Water elements merge at the inlet from the sea that fluctuates along with the ocean tide. The white shed also contains a small pier.

OPPOSITE A former water tower was stripped out and transformed into an illuminated sculpture or lighthouse. It is situated on an island that was created in order to save the original Banyan trees found there.

OPPOSITE TOP and BOTTOM The rail tracks that transported materials to the dockside have been cleared and restored to create a feature and path that runs for half a mile. This forms part of a network of paths that link different locations and exits.

RIGHT and BELOW The red steel box is a new design addition to create drama and a focus on the site, an outdoor room designed for the contemplation of China's cultural revolution. Zhongshan takes it name from its most famous son, the revolutionary leader Dr Sun Yatsen (Zhongshan is the Mandarin translation of his Cantonese name).

BELOW Red is a colour of great significance politically, but to the Chinese it also denotes health and prosperity.

"Today we interpret the use of public space in a new way and are able to focus on places that had no value twenty years ago."

Kathryn Gustafson

NEW TYPES OF SPACE

PREVIOUS PAGE A motorway flyover in Shanghai, China. Care has been taken to add planting at ground level to create a more pleasant route for pedestrians, but also, and more unusually, planters have been attached onto the sides of the motorway itself, presumably to provide a touch of nature for motorists as well.

LEFT Paris Plage Summer 2005. Every summer since 2002 the right side of the Seine between the Pont Neuf and Pont de Sully has been temporarily trans-formed into an urban beach complete with parasols, sun loungers, and sail-like banners to enhance the nautical feel.

AS OUR CITIES AND LIFESTYLES change, so do our definitions of public space as we claw back every available corner into the public domain, find new ways to spend our leisure time in the urban or non-urban environment, and demand more external spaces to be opened up. The result is that more imaginative, unusual types of public space are being created around us. The growth of community-led projects is creating public space that has very local and specific uses related to local needs and the physical qualities and features of their local environment.

These new spaces may have broader relevance and potential. Some spaces that we perceive as "public" are actually privately owned, as local authorities seek to offload places that they find difficult to manage and fund, or grant planning opportunities with caveats that a certain percentage of public space is created as part of the deal. Developers understand the value such spaces bring to their surrounding properties. These developer-owned spaces are "gifted" to the public and are open to them. There are often restrictions – I discovered this as I was driven away by a overzealous security guard for taking photographs; this was apparently against the rules, a ridiculous situation that, it seems, is not atypical. On the positive side, however, these spaces are generally of high quality and are well maintained, with good facilities such as cafés and bars and are also well used and liked by the public.

New types of spaces include the temporary and transient, spaces that are actually mobile and those that are almost invisible to those hurrying by. To create the great variety of all types then we have to become more flexible in how we view and define public space.

The aim of this chapter is to look at ways designers and community groups are pushing the boundaries of public space definition. The spaces here range from those that reclaim land for the public realm to those that reclaim water. This is a fascinating concept, the idea that a public space can be created – such as the floating Mur Island in Austria, where a space has "appeared" that links two rather disconnected sides of the city of Graz by inventing a new halfway location. This project treats the surface of the river as a new public venue. Obviously this type of project is costly, and would never have been commissioned without the impetus of the European City of Culture celebrations, which came with a desire to create a unique public space. However, it does show the imagination, and audacity that can be brought to the subject.

The open-air swimming pool in Copenhagen is a reinterpretation of a traditional public space, the lido, which fell out of favour in the late 20th century. All over Britain lidos, often excellent examples of Art Deco architecture, had been closing down, as they were costly to maintain and were falling out of use. There were many campaigns to save them, and this focused interest on them

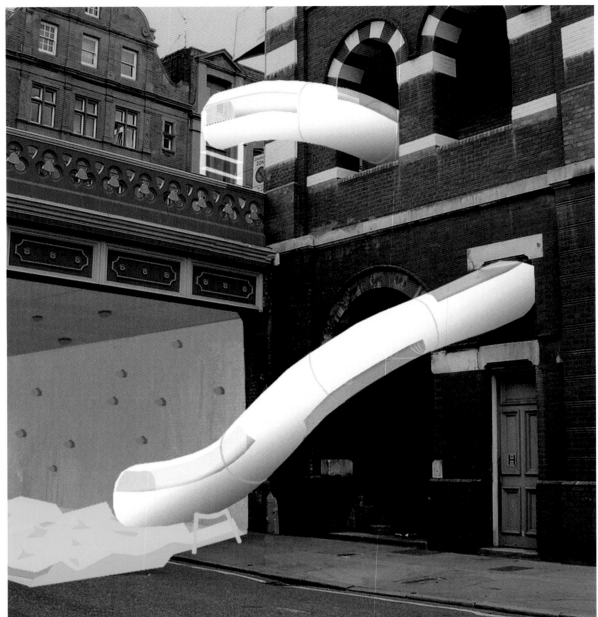

LEFT A competition idea by architect Christoph Zeller to transform an underpass in Clerkenwell, London. The plan is to create an adult play area, complete with giant slide, climbing wall, and swing, for the use of local workers who have little public space nearby.

once again. In Copenhagen the link between the pool and the park has created an impressive public space: it has proved that this typology can be popular even in a northern climate, and has reclaimed the harbour from commercial trade into a public amenity.

The Atlantic Road viewing platforms or beauty spots in Norway attracted me because it was an imaginative, yet simple, project that looked at the design possibilities of a type of space that is, to pardon the pun, overlooked. These little spaces exist in every country but are barely acknowledged or considered, their shape defined more by the wear and tear of cars and feet than any conscious design. This project demonstrates how to create spaces that give the visitor ample views and photo opportunities, and yet also protects the area by helping the visitor to understand how to negotiate this fragile interface between nature and tarmac. Most beauty spots are public-space eye_sores with their ugly street furniture; oversized, overflowing, and exposed rubbish bins; fading information boards; and prominent parking bays. In 3RW's USF Square, in Bergen, Norway, these elements actually contribute to the aesthetic experience and are attractive rather than intrusive. Essential tourist facilities, such as toilets, are also considered and, in one location, Eagleturn, benches double up as safety barriers.

Guerilla Gardening is not strictly a design project, but is about creating new types of public space: gardens and allotments from verges, construction sites, and any other patch of earth that is unloved or unclaimed. The design is the community action of reclaiming these as public spaces, drawing attention to them in the hope that they may be restored, or simply to raise the debate. The aesthetic is simply the pleasure anyone would experience seeing a muddy area transformed by a row of sunflowers, and speaks volumes about our yearning to see nature in an urban environment. It certainly questions the definition of public space.

The spontaneity and instant results such spaces can achieve also have a massive appeal. Forget the regeneration master plan, the public consultation, funding applications, and appeals – Guerrilla Gardening transformations happen with a trowel and some plants and take days rather than years. Many communities are weary of being consulted about options for their local public spaces and then waiting for years for something to happen, raising expectations which local authority

budgets and priorities cannot always meet. This is direct action in the most positive way. Although not providing long-term solutions, or the best way to approach larger areas of public space, these can be uplifting spaces for all and empowering for the community.

The artist collective of Greyworld has reacted against our visually dominant culture to create spaces that are altered, designed, or improved by sound. They create aural landscapes that transport us mentally, if only momentarily, to other locations and environments, or simply add some wit, lift our spirits, or make us smile in the way a bed of flowers might do in a park. This approach may require us to work or think a little in a public space, rather than passively accepting the experience.

The Youth Centre by SLA in Copenhagen, Denmark, shows an imaginative response to a brief for a small centre on contaminated land. Instead of using a large part of the

OPPOSITE A temporary summer installation in Broadgate, London, designed by AOC. It consists of a working, turf-covered bar. This area is also transformed into an ice rink during the winter.

RIGHT A temporary pavilion providing a raised viewing platform for public use on a main street in Clerkenwell, London. It was designed by 6a Architects in collaboration with fashion designers Eley Kishimoto for The Architecture Foundation.

being essentially two-dimensional, but to me it demonstrates a new thinking about the interaction of the public with their urban surroundings. It could so easily have been a wooden painted hoarding, giving away nothing to passers-by, but some effort and imagination has transformed a temporary inconvenience into a positive and welcome addition.

As our urban surroundings are constantly being demolished and rebuilt around us, often creating long-term eyesores, the pedestrian is left to negotiate barriers, roadworks, dust, and obstacle courses. The Green Green Screen demonstrates that much more thought could be given to such spaces, and that the public do deserve a better-quality experience when passing by.

And finally, along with the other projects in this chapter, the Green Green Screen also shows that design and imagination should be embedded into every detail that surrounds us in the public environment.

budget to remove the contaminated soil, they covered the whole site with a roofscape, which has become a new public space. This approach has created a far more interesting space than the client could have imagined, and wooden hills, a castle, and a skateboard park combined for the local youth community. This is, once again, about lateral thinking.

The Serpentine Pavilion project is a highly successful and slick example of a temporary public space, an area that is becoming increasingly popular. Because of its temporary nature, such schemes can often be more adventurous and experimental than permanent projects could hope to be, and attract wide interest as there is a "must see it before it goes" factor, and many normal public space issues such as maintenance and security are avoidable headaches.

The Green Green Hoarding in Tokyo may not appear to be a public space,

MUR ISLAND
Acconci Studio with Art & Idea
Graz, Austria (2003)

This project involves the creation of a new type of public space, by appropriating the surface of a river and creating a manmade "floating" island. The project was commissioned both to celebrate and be a main feature of Graz 2003, Cultural Capital of Europe, and was based on an idea by Robert Punkenhofer of Art & Idea.

Mur Island is a 550 tonne organically twisted series of steel shells, a design that investigates the relationship between public and private space. The island is built on a pontoon that lies on the riverbed, but can be floated in the event of a rise in water level. The shell houses an open-air theatre, and a café that turns into a bar at night nestles under the dome. In the twist between the bowl and the dome a children's playground landscape has been created. Vito Acconci, the artist who designed it, describes the concept: "People in the theatre see the playground in the background, whereas in the café the playground becomes part of the roof. These different functions should not be separated radically: as the water flows around the island we wanted to construct an object that is also flowing and changeable."

This new public space gives visitors fresh views of the city around it – and because of the lattice of glass windows the surroundings can be seen from deep within the artificial island. The project attracted over 500,000 visitors in the first six months of opening. According to Wolfgang Lorenz, the artistic director of Graz, "The project has created a positive awareness of the river which was previously rather unloved in Graz. It evens out the differences in importance between the two main areas of Graz by bridging the river between them with an object. This creates a place of unexpected experience in the middle of a thoroughly lively city, and a new landmark that attracts international attention."

ABOVE View of the island at night, an experience described by the artist Vito Acconci as "lying on the river like a spaceship". This new 930 sq m (1016 sq yd) public space can accommodate 350 people.

OPPOSITE A view of the open-air theatre space, the bridges linking the island to the shore, and the nearby footbridge. The lattice of steel and glass reflects the sun in a similar way to the water around it.

ABOVE The interior and exterior spaces flow into one another in an area that provides a link between the café space and the open-air theatre.

LEFT Originally the amphitheatre was to be set below water level so it looked like a "hole" in the water. Owing to cost concerns, however, the theatre was raised above the water line.

ABOVE

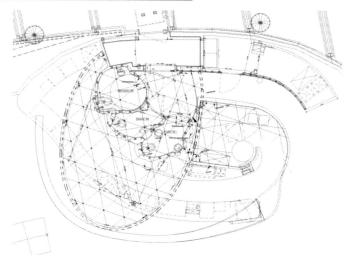

ABOVE The perspective section and plan of the island, demonstrating the complex construction. Acconci wanted the island to lie on the river like a spaceship.

RIGHT View of the wave-like theatre seating below a view of the café area, again reflecting the curves of the building and the movement of water. The palette is restricted to shades of blue and grey to create a harmonious design.

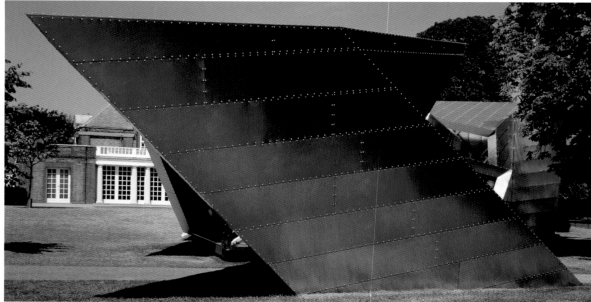

ABOVE, LEFT and BELOW The 2001 pavilion designed by Daniel Libeskind was entitled "Eighteen turns". Constructed from aluminium, it was conceived as "a lyrical counterpoint to Kensington Gardens and the Serpentine Gallery, a playful figure that weaves and stretches obliquely across space and this unique context".

SERPENTINE PAVILIONS
Various architects
Kensington Gardens, London (2000–)

Since 2000 the Serpentine Gallery, situated in Kensington Gardens in London, has nearly every year commissioned the building of a temporary summer pavilion on the lawn in front of the main gallery. The original pavilion, a tent-like structure by architect Zaha Hadid, was conceived as a one-off idea to celebrate the gallery's 30th anniversary in 2000, but proved such a draw – being the first structure by Hadid to be built in Britain, as well as a new park facility – that the decision was made to continue the project.

Each year (except 2004) a different leading international architect has designed a structure that acts as a café and events space, as well as a piece of sculpture and a visitor attraction. A prerequisite of the commission is that it must be the first structure designed by the architect in Britain, and this has added considerably to its appeal and press coverage.

Astutely, the gallery covers part of the cost of the pavilions by selling them on afterwards to rich collectors with large gardens, or institutions. The typology of the pavilion or temporary summer house for events in the park is a traditional Victorian one, but this had rather fallen out of fashion until the Serpentine came up with this idea.

Zaha Hadid's 2000 pavilion was followed by Daniel Liberskind in 2001, Toyo Ito in 2002, Oscar Niemeyer in 2003, and Alvaro Siza (with Eduardo Souto de Moura) in 2005.

The project, because of its smaller scale and more temporary nature, has allowed each architect to take a more radical approach to exploring what architecture can be, as there were fewer building constraints. Architecture is a difficult subject to convey with models and drawings in a traditional gallery context, so each of the pavilions acted as a complete architecture show.

The pavilions now stay in place for just three months, but the profile it has given the Serpentine has been huge, appealing to a non-gallery-visiting public, and attracting an additional 200,000 visitors in the first six weeks of opening. The project receives no public funding, relying instead on private sponsorship, but this also allows the gallery complete control of the project, enabling the commission to complement its regular exhibition programme of shows by leading contemporary artists.

ABOVE and LEFT The first pavilion designed by Iraqi Architect Zaha Hadid was a marquee-like tensile structure consisting of a PVC roof over a steel frame. After being dismantled, it was bought for use by the Royal Shakespeare Company as a summer events venue in Stratford.

ABOVE and RIGHT In Oscar Niemeyer's own words, the idea behind his 2003 pavilion "was to keep this project different, free, and audacious. This is what I prefer. I like to draw, I like to see from the blank sheet of paper a palace, a cathedral, the figure of a woman."

ABOVE The interior of the 2002 pavilion designed by the leading Japanese architect Toyo Ito. The project each year includes a café area, allowing the public to experience architecture in the most informal way.

ABOVE Toyo Ito's pavilion design is based on a box typology, systematically assembled by a pattern of intersecting lines with blade-like beams and columns. The apparently random scattering of lines across the structure is the product of an algorithm (a precise rule specifying how to solve a problem).

LEFT Toyo Ito's pavilion is constructed from white painted aluminium and glass. Like all the pavilions, the turnaround for the construction of the project, including solving all technical difficulties and ensuring that it is completed on time, is extremely tight.

LEFT The pleasant aroma of herbs and flowers and the cooling effect of the greenery on hot days make a welcome addition in a city that lacks green spaces for the public to enjoy.

GREEN GREEN SCREEN
Klein Dytham Architects
Tokyo, Japan (2003)

This may not initially seem like a public space, but it is a project that has completely transformed a streetscape and has made it a much more pleasant place to pass by.

The project was brought about by the need to construct a long hoarding to surround the site of a housing and retail development being carried out by Tadao Ando. The building work was going to last a long time – nearly three years – as a massive, six-storey basement needed to be dug out for car parking.

The mixed-use building by Ando was commissioned by the Mori Corporation, and the fact that mori means "forest" in Japanese gave the architects the germ of a concept. Klein Dytham Architects decided to create a living, growing hoarding that would provide visual relief on a busy retail street, using planting so that the screen would improve over the duration of the construction project it conceals.

The 274m (300yd) long screen is based on a traditional Japanese steel frame, onto which are bolted three layers of 2.5cm (1in) felt with pockets to hold the earth for plants. A hosepipe along the top trickles water down into the pockets to keep the plants moist, and there is a gutter that runs along the bottom to ensure that the pavement stays dry. The screen also has a vertical grass portion and is visually broken up with graphic wallpaper of plant images and, at one end, some advertising.

The advertising alone generates a staggering $100,000 every six weeks and this has made the project self-funding. About a third of the 13 different types of plants are replaced annually, such as the flowers, plus some herbs, partly because passers-by steal them for cooking (particularly the thyme). However, most are permanent, such as the ivys and grasses, and these have flourished. The screen will be removed in spring 2006.

LEFT The planting is broken up by information panels to help the public, including a map of the area and a list of shops. This is a major shopping area of Toyko, called Omotesando, and many premium brands are located nearby.

BELOW and BOTTOM The decorative graphic panels between the planting were designed by Namaiki graphic design company to blend in with the foliage, using similar colours and a natural theme. Klein Dytham decided the hoarding would look too heavy unless the greenery was broken up, a measure which also helped to reduce costs.

RIGHT and BELOW By law, Japanese hoardings have to be a standard 4m (13ft) high. There are also three access gates to the building sites – these are covered with graphics so that they blend in with the rest of the screen.

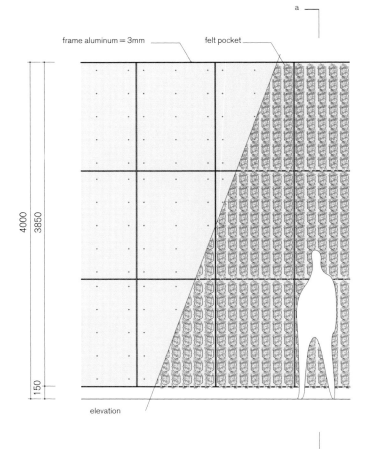

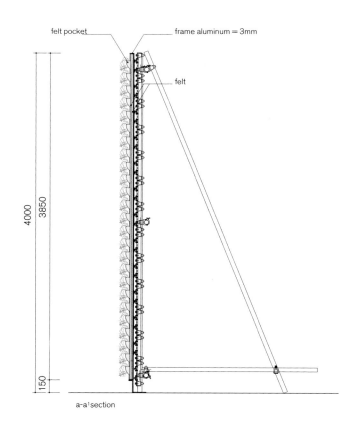

ABOVE The mix of grass, trailing leaves, and graphics adds texture and variety along the length of the huge screen. The hoarding is irresistable to the touch and also brings a smile to the faces of passers-by.

ABOVE A bird's-eye view of the pools, showing the main pool, the two smaller pools, and the diving tower to the left. The project is viewed as an extension of the park, which takes on the role of an urban "beach".

THE HARBOUR POOL
PLOT Architects
Copenhagen, Denmark (2003)

There had previously been a temporary pool on the site in Copenhagen where the Harbour Pool is now located. Because this had proved such a great success, PLOT Architects were commissioned to create a permanent version within a strict time schedule where both design and construction needed to take place over five months, and within a limited budget.

The temporary pool had been constructed as a floating island, accessed by a bridge, but this design created a bottleneck which resulted in queues and some overcrowding. PLOT decided to situate the new pool complex next to the recently created harbour park (replacing a former rail yard) where there are cafés and toilet facilities – this meant that it felt connected to the park and was directly accessible to anyone passing by. Visitors can now leave their towels and picnics on the grass in the park and stroll down to the pools to swim.

The size of the complex is dictated by the existing piles. It consists of two smaller pools, one with shallow water for small children and the other for youths. The main pool is without a constructed bottom as the harbour water is clean and monitored daily. The most striking feature is the diving tower, which offers three diving points and also provides a good viewing platform. The pools are surrounded by a stainless-steel railing design that rises at one point to form showers. The pools are open all the time and have proved immensely popular, so much so that they needed refurbishment after just two seasons.

This area of Copenhagen now has the highest real-estate value in the city, but before the creation of the harbour park six years ago and the pool in 2003 it used to have the lowest value.

The project is part of Copenhagen's Blue Plan, a policy that focuses on creating more projects on and near the water. Triathlon championships now take place in the pool, and both the park and the pool are the centre of local festivals and events. Julien de Smedt, a partner at PLOT, calls the complex "a little bit of Spain in Copenhagen", albeit one that still has a distinctly Scandinavian character.

LEFT A single lifeguard tower, with dramatic stripes, was positioned with a clear sightline of all three pools. This safety requirement dictated the design of the whole project.

BELOW The tight budget dictated a timber construction for all the main elements. The project is part of a plan to develop Copenhagen's 42km (26 miles) of wharf and docks: other proposed projects include space for houseboats, water sports, and promenades.

RIGHT Plans separating out the key elements in the design of the Baths: (from top) the sense of continuity with Islandsbrygge Harbour Park; the radial layout to ensure clear sightlines for the lifeguard; the long linear swimming pool for exercise; the paddling pool for children; accessibility for the disabled; and, finally, the complete picture.

BELOW A side view of the project, showing the crowds climbing the steps of the highly popular diving platform, from which there are three diving points. Bathing in the Copenhagen harbour carries no health risks as the water quality is constantly monitored.

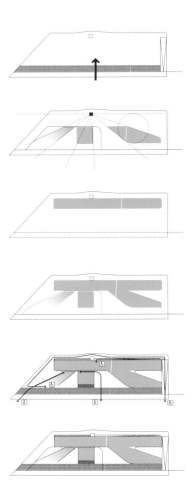

LEFT and BELOW The whole project was designed and constructed in just five months. The size of the pool was limited as the architects had to utilize the piles already existing in the water. The sharp angles were created from the need to have clear sightlines and also give the project a dynamic identity.

MARITIME YOUTH CENTRE
PLOT Architects
Sundby Harbour, Copenhagen, Denmark (2004)

The Maritime Youth Centre in Copenhagen is shared by two organizations, the youth centre itself and a sailing club, which uses the space to store its boats.

Because the site was polluted by heavy metals, the client stipulated that 25 per cent of the budget should be spent on soil decontamination. PLOT, the architects who were commissioned to undertake the project, felt that spending such a high proportion of a very tight budget on an "invisible" part of the project would be a waste. They solved the problem by using the same proportion of the budget to deck over the entire site of 2000 sq m (2392 sq yd) to cover the polluted, but stable, soil, therefore preventing any direct contact between the public and the earth. This gave PLOT the opportunity to create a far more interesting and dynamic space than the hut and cleared ground that had initially been envisaged by the client, and allowed the creation of a new type of public space using the new roofscape of the structure.

Dealt with in this way, the project also gave more space for the creation of the outdoor play area for children specified in the original brief. This outdoor area has also now become a popular promenade and viewing point for other local residents and visitors to the site.

By creating an undulating topography using the roofscape, space was created below in which to store the boats and construct a simple centre for youth events and meetings.

This low-maintenance project, constructed out of long-lasting hardwood, should age well and cost an incredibly reasonable 10 million crowns (£909,000). Situated in a run-down area of Copenhagen with a significant problem of youth-related crime, the Maritime Youth Centre has given an activity focus for local youths and a space in which they can express themselves constructively: they are encouraged to learn to sail and engage with nature.

During the winter the site has become popular for skateboarding, and as the roofscape has been designed as a loop, it has also been used as a BMX track. The project has won a number of awards, and on the back of the project's success the areas around the centre are being transformed into a new residential development.

ABOVE PLOT has created 37m (121ft) of indoor space and 400m (437yds) of outdoor space, which acts as a viewing platform to admire the seascape. The undulating topography is supported upon wooden piles.

LEFT The artificial landscape created is reminiscent of sand dunes. Copenhagen's coastline is undergoing a major phase of redevelopment, and with its dramatic view of the sea, the youth centre is in a prime position.

ABOVE The interior space of the youth centre has been kept simple so that it can be multi-functional, with a robust white terrazzo floor and a white concrete ceiling. The emphasis has been on the outside space, which acts as the main "room" for the centre.

LEFT Following the success of the youth centre, the architects designed a boardwalk for the sailing club in the same materials. The two interior spaces of the youth centre are visible here, one of which is used to store the sailing club's boats.

LEFT The wooden hills have become "castles" for the local children to defend, play mock battles on, and provide look-outs to spot pirates at sea. In the winter the snow-covered hills are used for snowboarding.

LEFT and BELOW Julien de Smedt, a partner at PLOT Architects, is a former skateboarder, so he knew how to design a space that would appeal to boarders. The spaces beneath the decks are used for storing canoes and bikes.

NORWEGIAN NATIONAL TOURIST ROADS
3RW Architects & Smedsvig Landskap
Norway (2005)

These are unusual public spaces, a series of viewing platforms at beauty spots along the Atlantic Sea Road and the Geiranger Trollstigen Road in Norway. This type of minor public space has rarely being given much attention or designed with the idea of being a contemporary and welcome addition to the landscape. Most similar spaces usually comprise a parking area, a cheap picnic bench, and an overflowing rubbish bin. Here,

these small but prominent public spaces have been designed to create a positive impact in their landscape. They contain many clever features, such as a rubbish shutes to underground bins to avoid refuse overflowing and benches that double as safety barriers.

These platforms were created as a part of an effort to strengthen the tourist industry in Norway's less urbanized areas. The aim was that by designing new viewpoints and

information areas the distinctive scenery that the road passes through could be highlighted.

3RW Architects and Smedsvig Landskap were commissioned by the road administration to design the different viewpoints, paths, outdoor furniture, and an information building along the road. Their innovative use of materials with a local significance – for example, a windbreak made of recycled tow rope from the fishing industry – became a way of creating new links between historical and natural values and tourism.

One of the projects, the viewing platform at Kjeksa, is located close to a small fishing village called Bud. It is constructed as a steel

framework pointing out towards the sea. It is unapologetically contemporary and shuns any faux nature trail overtones, while not intruding into a protected landscape.

The most stunning project is the circular white concrete platform at Eagle Turn, which juts out over the side of a mountain looking down to the ffjord below. A brave tourist can stand on a glass ledge and see the view directly beneath their feet.

All of the projects enhance the visitors' experience of this most dramatic landscape while protecting their safety and that of the environment.

OPPOSITE and BELOW A view and plan of Eagleturn, the most visited beauty spot by cruise ship-based tourists in Norway – over 400,000 come each year . Some 1400m (4593ft) below lies the Geiranger fjord. The precast concrete benches that border the road double up as safety barriers.

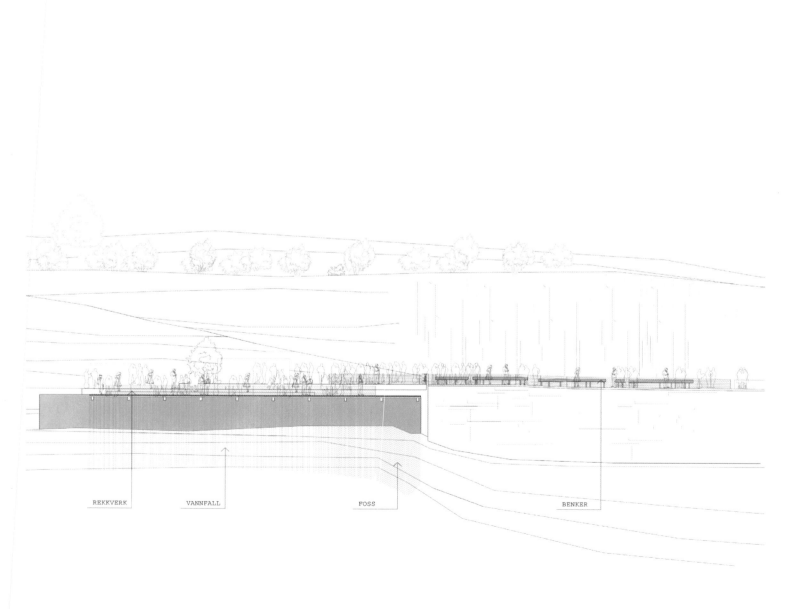

| REKKVERK | VANNFALL | FOSS | BENKER |

ABOVE The Askvagen viewing point is situated at the end of a jetty to provide the best sea views. The stone platform was constructed from a rock found on the road during a rockslide and was worked by hand to give it a rough finish. The steps were formed from a single sheet of Corten steel.

LEFT These public toilets at the Flydalsjuvet beauty spot near Geiranger have been built from the same logs used to make the traditional wooden Norwegian houses found in the local mountains. Though contemporary in design these conveniences fit into the context of the area.

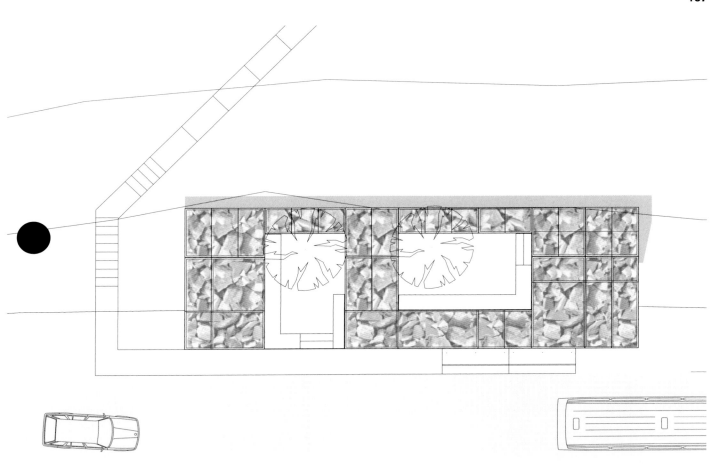

ABOVE and BELOW The viewpoint at Kjeksa overlooking the sea. The green gravel topping is a byproduct of the local smelting industry. Two old trees, clearly weathered by the harsh local climate, are used as central elements in the project. Under the platform there is a small garden where the public can sit. A small path of bright concrete leads from the viewpoint to the sea. It follows small variations in the landscape, creating a contrast with the unyielding, modern profile of the platform.

GUERRILLA GARDENING
Toronto Public Space Committee
Toronto, Canada (2002)

Guerrilla gardening is a simple yet effective way of utilizing neglected corners of our urban environment. Groups or individuals transform unloved corners of public spaces and plant them with anything from vegetables to flowers. The spaces can range from the bald squares of earth around trees in the street to abandoned building plots – any patch of earth that can be transformed by sprinkling a packet of seeds.

It is called "guerrilla gardening" because it is covert, unregulated, and done without permission, but it seems likely that it doesn't upset too many people, rather the reverse. As well as planting, the "guerrillas" monitor the spaces and carry on caring for them, such as watering when necessary or encouraging other locals to do so.

Guerrilla gardening is one of the many campaigns run by the Toronto Public Space Committee, an organization that lobbies the city on urban-environment issues and campaigns against the growing privatization of the public realm, particularly the growth of advertising on the streets. They call this type of gardening "graffiti with nature". The mission statement on their website states: "Without permission or licence we plant seeds and seedlings in all those neglected corners of public space. Join us as we vandalize the city with nature."

In the summer they organize weekly gardening sessions, identifying different locations around Toronto. In 2005, for example, they tackled empty concrete planters at the YMCA, an exposed corner of a construction site, and some tree planters, among many other projects.

Volunteers gather, armed with soil, water, seedlings, and a spoon. They encourage the use of native seeds, as non-native plants could be harmful or invasive to the surrounding eco-system and would then defeat their aims. The local police and Toronto's Parks and Recreational Department are, in the majority of cases, supportive. It is a novel and practical idea, which could be taken up by anyone, anywhere. We probably all pass a space every day that could be transformed with very little effort.

BELOW The bald areas of soil around the base of trees provide an excellent location for guerilla gardening, adding visual interest at ground level and discouraging dogs from soiling there.

ABOVE Benches and Bins project, Cambrdge 2005. These items of street furniture have been given human characteristics. They are even programmed to shiver in cold weather.

OPPOSITE TOP The artist Andrew Shoban of Greyworld describes the concept as "a flock of robotic benches and bins roaming around their own public space. The benches are social creatures and stick together whilst the bins are more solitary."

OPPOSITE BOTTOM The benches and bins were designed to be very heavy to discourage theft. All are fitted with Global Positioning System transmitters; if someone tried to remove them from the square an alarm would be activated.

VARIOUS PROJECTS
Greyworld
United Kingdom (1998–2005)

Greyworld is a group of artists that creates urban art in well-used spaces. Their primary objective is to create public art that allows people to become actively part of the creative process: the work isn't complete without them.

For the most part these installations are in the grey areas of the city. The work seeks to "short-circuit" both social and environmental expectations of the urban environment, actively lifting urban areas away from the banal and the ignored. Often the work isn't immediately visible, as their physical impact can be minimal.

"Railings", a project completed in Dublin in 1998 is a piece that is sculptural and functional in equal measure. Children like to pick up sticks and delight in running them along railings to create a noise. Here, Greyworld have installed some functional railings and tuned them so that when you run a stick along them they play "The Girl From Ipanema", which is guaranteed to raise a smile even on a rainy day. "Colour Stop Bus Stop", created in 2001 in Bradford, consists of five specially constructed bus shelters designed by architects Bauman Lyons – these are gently altered by the sound of a soothing female voice, which sings about the colour of the clothing of those waiting for buses. An award-winning project, it has been heralded as a unique and compelling way to alter the urban landscape.

Also in Dublin, "Bridge Two" was a temporary project where footsteps triggered sensors on a bridge to create the sounds of crunching snow, splashing through water, or walking through crunchy leaves, a nice way to transport people momentarily from an urban to a natural environment. A more recent ambitious project in Cambridge, which elevates functional street furniture into kinetic art, has seen the animation of bins and benches so that they wander around a public square – the bins gather around pedestrians like pigeons and line up to be emptied on rubbish-collection day. The gentle playfulness and humour evident in Greyworld are memorable and the way the pieces makes us look, listen, and question the role of the basic fabric and components of our urban environment offers us a realm of interesting and stimulating possibilities within our cities.

ABOVE LEFT One of five sculptural and colourful stop bus stops in Bradford (designed by architects Baumann Lyons in 2002). A female voice sings "The Colour of Song" to the passengers waiting for buses. The project won a Royal Society of Arts Art for Architecture Award.

ABOVE These ordinary looking railings were tuned to play "The Girl from Ipenama". This project is not flagged up by any signs, description, or provision of sticks — it has been left to the public to discover it themselves with their umbrella.

LEFT The Bridge Two Project in Dublin (completed in 2001) was a two-month-long installation created to celebrate the new millennium. As people walked across the bridge, sounds of crunching leaves, snow, and splashing through water were activated by sensors at foot level.

**PROJECT DATA
AND CONTACT
DETAILS**

NAME: FEDERATION SQUARE
(www.fedsq.com)
Location: Melbourne, Australia
Architect/Designer: Lab Architects
(www.labarchitecture.com)
Size: 3.8ha
Budget: $450 million

Lab Architecture Studio
Level 4 325 Flinders lane
Melbourne 3000
Australia

Federation Square Management
CNR Swanston & Flinders Streets
Melbourne 3000
Australia

NAME: BLUE CARPET
Location: Newcastle, UK
Architect/Designer: Thomas Heatherwick
(www.thomasheatherwick.com)
Size: 2500 sq m (whole square) 1500 sq m
(area of blue carpet)
Budget: £1.2 million

Thomas Heatherwick Studio
16 Acton Street
London WC1X 9NG
UK

Photographer: Mark Pinder
Email: pinder.photo@btinternet.com

NAME: CHASSE TERREIN
Location: Breda city centre, The Netherlands
Architect/Designer: West 8 (www.west8.nl)
Size: 15ha

West 8 Urban Design & Landscape Architecture
PO Box 24326
3007 DH Rotterdam
The Netherlands

NAME: USF SQUARE
Location: Bergen, Norway
Architect/Designer: 3RW Architects
(www.3RW.no)
Landscape Architect: Smedsvig Landskap
Architects AS
Completed: June 2003
Commissioned by: USF Art Center,
Norwegian Preserving Company AS (NPC
AS), Bergen Building Company (BOB), and
Bergen Municipality.

Consultant/constructional engineer: NODE
Rådgivende ingeniører AS
Contractors: Børø Stål AS, Nature AS,
Betonggulv AS
Project management and administration: BOB
Size: 2000 sq m

3RW Architects (www.3rw.no)
PB 1131
5809 Bergen
Norway

NAME: STORTORGET SQUARE
Location: Kalmer, Sweden
Architect/Designer: Caruso St John
(www.carusostjohn.com); underground
fountains and the red lights on masts were
the result of colloboration with Eva Löfdahl.
Size: 16,000 sq m
Budget: £1 million

Caruso St John Architects
1 Coate Street
London E2 9AG
UK

Photographer: Hélène Binet
Email: helenebinet@lycos.com

NAME: TILLA DURIEUX PARK
Location: Potsdamer Platz, Berlin, Germany
Architect/Designer: DS Landscape Architects
(www.ds.landscapearchitects.nl)
Size: 2.5ha
Client: Mitte Municipal District, Berlin
Head contractor: Fa. Otto Kittel GmbH, Berlin
Subcontractors: Original Kinderland, Geeste

DS Landscape Architects
Overtoom 197
1054 HT Amsterdam
The Netherlands

NAME: HENRIETTA PARK
Location: Potsdamer Platz, Berlin, Germany
Architect/Designer: DS Landscape Architects
(www.ds.landscapearchitects.nl)
Area: 1ha

DS Landscape Architects
Overtoom 197
1054 HT Amsterdam
The Netherlands

NAME: MARKETPLACE
Location: Stuttgart, Germany
Architect: Dietrich Brennenstuhl/Nimbus
Design GmbH (www.nimbus-design.com)
Lighting concept and realization: Dietrich
Brennenstuhl and Markus Mohn
Luminaire design: Susanne Wolf,
Markus Mohn
Size: 6500 sq m

Nimbus Design GmbH
Sieglesstraße 41
D-70469
Stuttgart
Germany

NAME: PARK JB LEBAS
Location: Lille Park, France
Architect/Designer: West 8 (www.west8.nl)

West 8 Urban Design & Landscape Architecture
PO Box 24326
3007 DH Rotterdam
The Netherlands

NAME: RAPONGGI SEATING
(www.mori.art.museum/html/eng/artanddesi
gnmap/)
Location: Tokyo, Japan
Architect/Designer: Various – Louise
Bourgeois, Isa Genzken, Choi Jeong Hwa,
Martin Puryear, Sol Lewitt, Miyajima Tatsuo,
Miura Jeiko, Cai Guo-Qiang, Droog Design,
Jasper Morrison, Hibino Katsuhiko, Uchida
Shigeru, Andrea Branzi, Ito Toyo, Ettore
Sottsass, Yoshioka Tokujin, Ron Arad, Thomas
Sandell, Karim Rashid

Mori Art Museum
Roppongi Hills Mori Tower
6-10-1 Roppongi
Minato-ku
Tokyo 106-6150
Japan

Photographer: Satoshi Asakawa
Email: jahtosh@d1.dion.ne.jp

NAME: PASEO DE OVALO, TERUEL
Location: Teruel, Spain
Architect/Designer: David Chipperfield
(www.davidchipperfield.co.uk) in association
with b720 Arquitectura.
Size: 7215 sq m
Budget: £3.9 million

David Chipperfield Architects
Cobham Mews
Agar Grove
London NW1 9SB
UK

Photographer: Hisao Susuki
Email: hisao.suzuki@teleline.es

NAME: MEMORIAL BRIDGE
Location: Rijeka, Croatia
Architect/Designer: 3LHD (www.3LHD.com)
Project team: 3LHD – Silvije Novak, Marko
Dabrovic, Sasa Begovic, Tanja Grozdanic,
Sinisa Glusica, with Koraljka Brebric,
Milan Strbac
Structural engineers: CES doo Rijeka (Jean
Wolf, Zoran Novacki, Dusan Srejic), UPI-2M
doo Zagreb, Berislav Medic
Main Contractors: GP Krk (general), Shipyard
3.Maj (steel construction), Almes (aluminium,
glass), Ribaric (lighting)
Collaborators: B Jurjevic (Almes), M Lindquist
(SAPA aluminium), NOVA Karlovac (square
and memorial surface), Carpentry Rudolf
(benches, handrail), Aljosa Sribar (OSRAM
LED), Ciril Zlobec (glass prisms)
Client: City of Rijeka, Croatia
Completed: 2001

3LHD
Varsavska 8/1
HR-10000
Zagreb
Croatia

**NAME: ZUTPHEN CITY CENTRE
IMPROVEMENTS**
Location: Zutphen,
Architect/Designer: Okra Landscape
Architects (www.okra.nl)

Okra Landscape Architects
Oudegracht 23
3511 AB Utrecht
The Netherlands

NAME: THE EASTBANK ESPLANADE
Location: Portland, Oregon, US
Architect/Designer: MayerReed
(www.mayerreed.com)
Budget: $30million
Size: 4.8km

Mayer Reed
319 SW Washington, Suite 820
Portland, Oregon, 97204
USA

NAME: FUZI PEDESTRIAN ZONE
Location: San Candido/Innichen, Austria
Architect/Designer: AllesWirdGut
  (www.alleswirdgut.cc)
Size: 3.6ha
Budget: 570,000 euros

AllesWirdGut
Große Neugasse 27
1040 Vienna
Austria

Photographer: Hertha Hurnaus
Email: hehu@hurnaus.com

NAME: LIFFEY BOARDWALK
Location: Dublin, Ireland
Architect/Designer: McGarry Ni Eanaigh
  Architects (www.mcgnie.ie)
Size: 650 m

McGarry Ni Eanaigh Architects
21 Laurence Street
Drogheda
County Louth
Ireland

Photographer: Barry Mason
Email: bmasonphoto@eircom.net

NAME: SOUTH-EASTERN COASTAL PARK
Location: Barcelona, Spain
Architect/Designer: Foreign Office Architects
  (www.f-o-a.net)
Size: 50,000 sq m
Budget: 12 million euros

Foreign Office Architects
55 Curtain Road
London
EC2A 3PT

Photographer: Ramon Pratt, Actar, Barcelona
Email: info@actar-mail.com

NAME: MILLENNIUM PARK
  (www.milleniumpark.org)
Location: Chicago, US
Architect/Designer: Various, including Frank

Gehry, Anish Kapoor, Jaume Plensa. The Lurie
Garden was designed by Kathryn Gustafson,
Jennifer Guthrie and Shannon Nichol
(www.ggnltd.com)
Size: 10ha
Budget: $450 million

NAME: LANDFORM UEDA
(www.edinburgharchitecture.co.uk/landform_ch
arles_jencks.htm)
Location: Museum of Modern Art, Edinburgh,
  Scotland
Architect/Designer: Charles Jencks in
  collaboration with Terry Farrell & Partners
Budget: £380,000
Area of water: 1622 sq m
Volume of water: 2000 cu m
Maximum depth of water: 1.2 m
Volume of excavations: 4000 cu m
**Volume of imported shale for shaping
  landform:** 3476 cu m

Charles Jencks
www.charlesjencks.com

Terry Farrell & Partners
www.terryfarrell.co.uk

The National Galleries of Scotland
www.nationalgalleries.org

Photographer: Allan Forbes
Email: allan.forbes@onetel.com

Photographer: Keith Hunter
Email: keith@khp.demon.co.uk

Photographer: Glynn Satterley
Email: info@glynsatterley.com

NAME: DANIA PARK
Location: Malmo, Sweden
Client: City of Malmo, Sweden
Architect/Designer: Thorbjorn Andersson
  and PeGe Hillinge, FFNS Architects
  (www.sweco.se)
Size: 20,000 sq m
Budget: 4.5 million euros
Completed: 2002

SWECO FFNS Landscape Architects
Nackagatan 4
Box 17920, 118 95 Stockholm
Sweden

NAME: THE ANCHOR PARK
Location: Malmo, Sweden
Architect/Designer: SLA Landscape
Architects (www.sla.dk)
Budget: 4 million euros

SLA Landscape Architects
Vaerkstedmagasinet
Refshalevej A 153
DK 1432 Copenhagen K

NAME: COLUMBINE GARDEN
Location: Tivoli Gardens, Copenhagen,
Denmark
Architect/Designer: SLA Landscape
Architects (www.sla.dk)

SLA Landscape Architects
Vaerkstedmagasinet
Refshalevej A 153
DK 1432 Copenhagen K
Denmark

NAME: SWINDLER COVE PARK
Location: New York, USA
Architect/Designer: New York Restoration
Project (www.nyrp.org)
Size: 2ha

New York Restoration Project
31 West 56th Street
New York, NY 10019
USA

NAME: WESTBLAAK SKATEPARK
Location: Rotterdam, The Netherlands
Architect/Designer: dS+V
(www.dsv.rotterdam.nl); manager's container
by BAR Architects (Joost Glissenaar); skate
objects by Solos International (Jerry Beckers);
pavement graphic design by 75B
Size: 6700 sq m
Budget: 1.8 million euros

dS+V, Gemeente Rotterdam
Galvanistraat 15
3029 AD Rotterdam
Postbus 6699
3002 AR Rotterdam
The Netherlands

NAME: WESTERGASFABRIEK PARK
Location: Amsterdam, The Netherlands
Architect/Designer: Kathryn Gustafsen

of Gustafson-Porter (www.gustafson-
porter.com)
Budget: 15 million euros

Gustafson Porter
Unit D, Linton House
39–51 Highgate Road
London NW5 1RS
UK

NAME: A13 ARTSCAPE PROJECT
(www.lbbd.gov.uk/4-arts-
culture/a13/a13artscape-menu.html)
Location: London, UK
Architect/Designer: Various – Tom de Paor,
Clare Brew, Anu Patel, Jason Cornish, Phil
Power, Rob Kesseler, Graham Ellard, Stephen
Johnstone, Pat Kaufman, MUF
Architecture/Art, Rayna Nadeem, Thomas
Heatherwick Studio, Kinnear Landscape
Architects, Andrew Darke, Studio 3 Arts, East
London Dance, Arc Theatre
Budget: £10 million
Client/Commisioning Body: London
Borough of Barking & Dagenham

Arts Service
Learning & Cultural Services
London Borough of Barking & Dagenham
Westbury Centre
Ripple Road
Barking IG11 7PT
UK

www.barking-dagenham.gov.uk

NAME: THE NATURE PLAYGROUND
Location: Valby Park, Denmark
Architect/Designer: Helle Nebelong
(www.sansehaver.dk); towers designed by
students at The Danish School of Design –
Kirsten Due Kongsbach, Pernille Frank Dige,
Pernille Bustrup, Fridrik Bjarnason
Civil engineer: NCC Construction
Denmark A/S
Construction manager: Bjarne Hansen
Size: 20,000 sq m
Budget: _c._ £800,000

Helle Nebleong
Landscape Architect MAA, MDL, MPM
Jaegersborg Allé 227 st tv
2820 Gentofte
Denmark

Contact: Helle Nebelong
Email: hellenebelong@hotmail.com

NAME: THE SOWETO MOUNTAIN OF HOPE (SOMOHO)
Location: Soweto, South Africa
Architect: Amandla Waste Creations and The Hub Collective
Co-ordinators/designers: Mandla Mentoor, Katy Marks, and Hillary Lindsay
Contributors: The Tshiawelo community, Soweto
Support: Ian Bonhote, John Clarke, Gaia Foundation, Lucy Hinton, Dr Colin Hudson, Peter Khomane, Jonathan Robinson, Roots and Shoots, Refiloe Serota, Christian de Sousa
Principal funders: The British High Commission, Canadian High Commission, Development Bank of South Africa ... and many others who have given time, energy, and money.

Contact the hub collective in the UK:
katy.marks@the-hub.net
www.the-hub.net www.the-hub.net
somoho in South Africa:
e-mail: somoho@mail.ngo.za

NAME: ZHONGSHAN SHIPYARD
Location: Qijiang Park, Zhongshan, China
Architect/Designer: Turenscape (www.turenscape.com/English) and the Centre for Landscape Architecture at Beijing University

Turenscape
ZhongguanCun FaZhan DaSha
12 ShangDi Xinxi Lu
HaiDian District
Beijing PR
China 100085

NAME: MUR ISLAND
Location: Graz, Austria
Architect/Designer: Acconci Studio (www.acconci.com) with Art & Idea
Size: 3142 sq m
Engineers: Zenckner & Handl, Kurt Kratzer
Contractors: SFL

Acconci Studio
20 Jay Street #215
Brooklyn, NY 11201
USA

NAME: SERPENTINE PAVILION
(www.serpentinegallery.org)
Location: London, UK
Architect/Designer: Various – Zaha Hadid (2000), Daniel Libeskind with Arup (2001), Toyo Ito with Arup (2002), Oscar Niemeyer (2003), Alvaro Siza and Eduardo Souto de Moura with Cecil Balmond (2005)
Civil Engineer: Arup Associates

Serpentine Gallery
Kensington Gardens
London W2 3XA

NAME: GREEN GREEN SCREEN
Location: Tokyo, Japan
Architect/Designer: Klein Dytham Architecture (www.klein-dytham.com)

Klein Dytham Architecture
Deluxe 1-3-3 Azabu Juban
Minato ku
Tokyo 106 0045
Japan

NAME: OPEN-AIR SWIMMING POOL HAVNEBADET (HARBOUR BATH)
Location: Kobenhavn, Denmark
Architect/Designer: PLOT (www.plot.dk)
Size: 1600 sq m
Budget: 520 000 euros

PLOT
Vesterbrogade 69D 2SAL
Baghuset 1620 KBHV
Denmark

NAME: MARITIME YOUTH CENTRE
Location: Amager, Denmark
Architect/Designer: PLOT (www.plot.dk)
Size: 2000 sq m
Budget: 1.17 million euros

PLOT
Vesterbrogade 69D 2SAL
Baghuset 1620 KBHV
Denmark

NAME: ATLANTIC ROAD VISITOR SPOTS
Location: Kjeksa, The Atlantic Road, and Romsdal, Norway
Architect/Designer: 3RW Architects (www.3rw.no)

Landscape Architect: Smedsvig Landskap AS
Engineer: Node AS

3RW Architects
PB 1131
5809 Bergen
Norway

NAME: GUERRILLA GARDENING
Location: Toronto, Canada
Architect/Designer: Toronto Public
    Space Committee
    (http://publicspace.ca/gardeners.htm)

NAME: VARIOUS GREYWORLD
    PROJECTS
Name: Railings
Location: Paris
Completed: 1996
Name: Bridge 2
Location: Millennium Bridge, Dublin
Completed: 2000

Name: ColourStops
Location: Bradford, UK
Architect/Designer: Greyworld
    (www.greyworld.org) and bus shelters
    designed by Baumen Lyons Associates
    (www.baumanlyons.co.uk)
Completed: 2002

Name: Bins & Benches
Location: Cambridge, UK
Completed: 2004

Greyworld
10 Wilkes Street
London E1 6QF
UK

FURTHER READING

Publications:

Amidon, J, *Radical Landscapes: Reinventing Outdoor Space,* Thames & Hudson, London, 2001

Amidon, J, *Moving Horizons: The Landscape Architecture of Kathryn Gustafson & Partners,* Birkhäser, Switzerland, 2005

Billingham, J & Cole, R, *The Good Place Guide: Urban Design in Britain & Ireland,* Batsford, London, 2002

Conway, H, *Public Parks,* Shire Publications Ltd, UK, 1996

Cooper Marcus, C & Francis C (ed), *People Places: Design Guidelines for Urban Open Space,* John Wiley & Sons Inc, Canada, 1998

Fieldhouse, K & Woudstra, J (ed), *The Regeneration of Public Parks,* E & FN Spon, London, 2000

Gastil, RW, & Ryan, Z (ed), *Open: New Designs for Public Space,* Van Alen Institute, New York, 2004

Gehl, J & Gemzoe, L, *New City Spaces,* The Danish Architectural Press, Copenhagen, 2003

Hare, C, *Landscape London: A Guide to Recent Gardens, Parks and Urban Spaces,* Ellipsis, London, 2001

Hill, P, *Contemporary History of Garden Design: European Gardens between Art and Architecture,* Birkhäser, Switzerland, 2004

Holden, R, *New Landscape Design,* Laurence King Publishing, London, 2003

Koekebakker, O, *Westergasfabriek Culture Park: Transformation of a Former Industrial Site in Amsterdam,* Nai Publishers, Rotterdam, 2003

Nicolin, P & Repishti, F (ed), *Dictionary of Today's Landscape Designers,* Skira, Italy, 2003

Richardson, T (ed), *The Vanguard Landscapes and Gardens of Martha Scwartz,* Thames & Hudson, London, 2004

Acconci, V/Acconci Studio, *Building an Island: Mur Island, Graz/Austria,* Hatje Cantz Verlag, Germany, 2003

Art, Design and the City: Roppongi Hills Public Art Project 1, Mori Art Museum Publications, Japan, 2004

Con_Con: Constructed Connections 2004 Realisation, Verlag Silke Schreiber, Munich, 2004

Henriette-Herz-Park, Potsdamer Platz Berlin, Shlomo Koren & DS Landscape Architects Publication, Amsterdam, 2002

Landscape Architecture in Scandinavia, Topos (ed), Birkhäuser/Callwey, Germany, 2002

Parks: Green Urban Spaces in European Cities, Topos (ed), Birkhäuser/Callwey, Germany, 2002

Small Structures: Exemplary Projects for Town and Landscape, Topos (ed), Birkhäuser/Callwey, Germany, 2004

The Netherlands in Focus: Exemplary Ideas and Concepts for Town and Landscape, Topos (ed), Birkhäuser/Callwey, Germany, 2002

Tilla-Durieux-Park, Potsdamer Platz Berlin, DS Landscape Architects Publication, Amsterdam, 2003

Urban Squares: Recent European Promenades, Squares and City Centres, Topos (ed), Birkhäuser/Callwey, Germany, 2002

West 8, Skira, Italy, 2000

Topos European Landscape Magazine

WEBSITES:

www.cabe.org.uk
www.cabespace.org.uk
www.designtrust.org
www.eura.org
www.green-space.org.uk
www.legepladsen.org
www.livingstreets.org.uk
www.pps.org
www.topos.de
www.vanalen.org
www.veipark.kk.dk/publikationer/pdf/050_Valbyparken.pdf

PHOTOGRAPHIC CREDITS

FOREWORD
p6 – EDAW/Photography by Dixi Carrillo

INTRODUCTION
p8 – Turenscape
p11 – Dominic Papa
p12 – Copyright: SLA/Photo: Torben Petersen
p13 – Copyright: SLA/Photo: Lars Gundersen
p14 – NYRP
p15 – Gustafson Porter

ESSAY ONE
p16 – Copyright: SLA/Photo: Jens Lindhe
p18 – Sarah Gaventa
p20 – Dominic Papa
p21 – Sarah Gaventa
p23 – Sarah Gaventa

FEDERATION SQUARE
p24 – Photography: John Gollings/Copyright: Federation Square Management
p25t – Photography: Peter Clarke/Copyright: Federation Square Management
p25b – Photography: Peter Clarke / Copyright: Federation Square Management
p26/27 Photography: John Gollings/Copyright: Federation Square Management

BLUE CARPET
p28 – Mark Pinder
p29tl – Mark Pinder
p29tr – Mark Pinder
p29b – Mark Pinder

CITY CENTRE, BREDA
p30 – West 8
p31b – Sarah Gaventa
p32t – Sarah Gaventa
p32b – Sarah Gaventa
p33t – Sarah Gaventa
p33bl – Sarah Gaventa
p33br – Sarah Gaventa

USF SQUARE
p34t – 3RW Architects
p34br – 3RW Architects
p35 – 3RW Architects

STORTORGET SQUARE
p36/37 – Helene Binet
p38tl – Helene Binet
p38tr – Helene Binet
p38b – Photography: Adam Caruso / Copyright: Caruso St. John
p39 – Helene Binet

TILLA DURIEUX PARK
p40 – Jens Schulz
p41t – Hanns Joosten
p41b – DS Landscape Architects
p42t – Aeliane van den Ende

p42m – DS Landscape Architects & Unknown Photographer
p42b – DS Landscape Architects & Unknown Photographer
p43 – Jens Schulz

HENRIETTA PARK
p44t – DS Landscape Architects
p44ml – DS Landscape Architects
p44mr – DS Landscape Architects
p44b – DS Landscape Architects
p45t – Daniel Koning
p45ml – Daniel Koning
p45mr – DS Landscape Architects
p45b – DS Landscape Architects

MARKETPLACE
p46l – Photography: Jens Kusters / Copyright: Nimbus Design GmbH
p46tr – Photography: Jens Kusters / Copyright: Nimbus Design GmbH
p46br – Photography: Jens Kusters / Copyright: Nimbus Design GmbH
p47 – Photography: Jens Kusters / Copyright: Nimbus Design GmbH

ESSAY TWO
p48 – Dominic Papa
p50l – Steve Speller
p50r – Steve Speller
p51 – Steve Speller
p52 – Dominic Papa
p53 – Courtesy Pearson Lloyd
p55t – Sarah Gaventa
p55b – Sarah Gaventa

THE ROPPONGI HILLS PROJECT
p56 – Mori Arts Museum
p57t – Mori Arts Museum
p57m – Mori Arts Museum
p57b – Mori Arts Museum
p58t – Satoshi Asakawa
p58m – Satoshi Asakawa
p58b – Mori Arts Museum
p59t – Satoshi Asakawa
p59b – Satoshi Asakawa

PLENUA PASEO TEURAL
p60 – Hisao Suzuki
p61 – Hisao Suzuki
p62l – 981-16.jpg Hisao Suzuki
p62tr – Hisao Suzuki
p62br – Hisao Suzuki
p63 – Hisao Suzuki

MEMORIAL BRIDGE
p64 – Photography: Aljosa Brajdic / Copyright: 3LHD
p65tl – 3LHD
p65tm – 3LHD
p65tr – 3LHD

p65m – 3LHD
p65b Photography: Aljosa Brajdic / Copyright: 3LHD
p66t – 3LHD
p66b Photography: Aljosa Brajdic / Copyright: 3LHD
p67t – 3LHD
p67b – Photography: Aljosa Brajdic / Copyright: 3LHD
p68t – 3LHD
p68b – Photography: Aljosa Brajdic / Copyright: 3LHD
p69l – Photography: Aljosa Brajdic / Copyright: 3LHD
p69tr – Photography: Aljosa Brajdic / Copyright: 3LHD
p69br – 3LHD

ZUTPHEN STREETSCAPE
p70tl – OKRA
p71tr – OKRA
p71tl – OKRA
p71tr – OKRA
p71b – OKRA

EASTBANK ESPLANADE
p72 – Copyright: Bruce Forster
p74tl – Copyright: Bruce Forster
p74tr – Copyright: Bruce Forster
p74b – Copyright: Bruce Forster
p75t – Copyright: Bruce Forster
p75bl – Copyright: Bruce Forster
p75br – Copyright: Bruce Forster

FUZI PEDESTRIAN ZONE
p76/77 – Hertha Hurnaus
p78b – Hertha Hurnaus
p78t – Hertha Hurnaus
p79b – Hertha Hurnaus
p79t – Hertha Hurnaus
p80b – Hertha Hurnaus
p80t – Hertha Hurnaus
p81b – Hertha Hurnaus
p81tl – Hertha Hurnaus
p81tr – AWG
p81b – Hertha Hurnaus

LIFFY BOARDWALK
p82l – Barry Mason Photographer
p82r – Mc Garry Ni Eanaigh Architects
p83t – Barry Mason Photographer
p83bl – Barry Mason Photographer
p83br – Barry Mason Photographer

ESSAY THREE
p84 – Maria Moore
p87 – Dominic Papa
p88 – Belinda Lawley
p89 – Dominic Papa
p90 – Sarah Gaventa
p91l – Belinda Lawley
p91r – Belinda Lawley

SOUTH EASTERN COASTAL PARK
p92/93 – Courtesy FOA
p94t – Ramon Prat, Actar, Barcelona

p94tm – Ramon Prat, Actar, Barcelona
p94bm – Ramon Prat, Actar, Barcelona
p94tb – Ramon Prat, Actar, Barcelona
p94b – Ramon Prat, Actar, Barcelona
p95t – Ramon Prat, Actar, Barcelona
p95b – Ramon Prat, Actar, Barcelona

MILLENNIUM PARK
p96 – City of Chicago/Peter J. Schulz
p97 – Caroline O'Boyle/Chicago Park District
p98t – Gustafson Guthrie Nichol Ltd
p98m – Gustafson Guthrie Nichol Ltd
p98b – Gustafson Guthrie Nichol Ltd
p99t – City of Chicago/Peter J. Schulz
p99b – City of Chicago/Mark Montgomery
p100t – City of Chicago/Peter J. Schulz
p100m – Caroline O'Boyle/Chicago Park District
p100b – City of Chicago/Chris McGuire
p100br – Gustafson Guthrie Nichol Ltd
p101t – Gustafson Guthrie Nichol Ltd
p101m – Gustafson Guthrie Nichol Ltd
p101b – Gustafson Guthrie Nichol Ltd

LANDFORM PROJECT
p102 – Keith Hunter
p103t – Allan Forbes
p103m – Keith Hunter
p103b – Phtography/Copyright: Glyn Satterley

DANIA PARK
p105 – Photography: Ake E:son Lindman / Copyright: SWECO FFNS
p106tl – Photography: Lena Ason / Copyright: SWECO FFNS
p106tr – Photography: Ingvar Andersson / Copyright: SWECO FFNS
p106b – Photography: Ingvar Andersson / Copyright: SWECO FFNS
p107t – Photography: Ake E:son Lindman / Copyright: SWECO FFNS
p107b – Photography: Ulf Celander / Copyright: SWECO FFNS
p108t – Photography: Jens Linde / Copyright: SWECO

FFNS
p108b – Photography: Ulf
   Celander / Copyright:
   SWECO FFNS
p109 – Photography: Jens Linde
   / Copyright: SWECO FFNS

ANCHOR PARK
p110 – Copyright: SLA/Photo:
   Torben Petersen
p111 – Copyright: SLA
   Landskabsarkiteter
p112tl – Copyright: SLA/Photo:
   Torben Petersen
p112tr – Copyright: SLA/Photo:
   Torben Petersen
p112m – Copyright: SLA
   Landskabsarkiteter/Photo:
   Torben Petersen
p112b – Copyright: SLA
   Landskabsarkiteter
p113 – Copyright: SLA
   Landskabsarkiteter/Photo:
   Jens Lindhe

COLUMBINE GARDEN
p114/115 – Copyright:
   SLA/Photo: Torben Petersen
p116/117 – Copyright:
   SLA/Photo: Torben Petersen

SWINDLER COVE PARK
p118t – NYRP
p118m – NYRP
p118b – NYRP

PARK J B LEBAS
p120 – West 8
p121t – Copyright: West 8
p121b – Sarah Gaventa
p122t – Sarah Gaventa
p122m – Sarah Gaventa
p122b – Sarah Gaventa
p123 – Sarah Gaventa

ESSAY FOUR
p124 – Sarah Gaventa
p127 – Gustafson Porter
p128 – Sarah Gaventa
p129 – dS+V
p131 – Turenscape

WESTBLAAK SKATEPARK
p132 – Copyright: dS+V
p133 – dS+V
p133 – dS+V
p134 – Sarah Gaventa
p134 – Sarah Gaventa
p134/5 – Sarah Gaventa
p135 – Sarah Gaventa

**WESTERGASFABRIEK
CULTURE PARK**
p136 – Courtesy Gustafson
   Porter Landscape Architects
p136 – Courtesy Gustafson
   Porter Landscape Architects
p136 – Courtesy Gustafson
   Porter Landscape Architects
p137 – Courtesy Gustafson
   Porter Landscape Architects
p137 – Courtesy Gustafson
   Porter Landscape Architects

p138 – Courtesy Gustafson
   Porter Landscape Architects
p138 – Courtesy Gustafson
   Porter Landscape Architects
p139 – Courtesy Gustafson
   Porter Landscape Architects
p139 – Courtesy Gustafson
   Porter Landscape Architects
p139 – Courtesy Gustafson
   Porter Landscape Architects

**ARTERIAL A13 ARTSCAPE
PROJECT**
p140t – Douglas Atfield &
   London Borough of Barking &
   Dagenham Arts Service
p140m – Douglas Atfield &
   London Borough of Barking &
   Dagenham Arts Service
p140/141b – Photography/
   Copyright: Douglas Atfield &
   London Borough of Barking &
   Dagenham Arts Service
p142/143t – Paul Bookless &
   London Borough of Barking &
   Dagenham Arts Service
p142m – Douglas Atfield &
   London Borough of Barking &
   Dagenham Arts Service
p142b – PB's Paul Bookless &
   London Borough of Barking &
   Dagenham Arts Service
p143 – Douglas Atfield &
   London Borough of Barking &
   Dagenham Arts Service

NATURE PLAYGROUND
p144/145 – Helle Nebelong
p146tl – Helle Nebelong
p146tr – Helle Nebelong
p146b – Helle Nebelong
p147tl – Helle Nebelong
p147tr – Helle Nebelong
p147b – Helle Nebelong

**SOMOHO MOUNTAIN OF
HOPE**
p148l – Johannesburg
   Metropolitan Council
p148r – Ito & Katy Marks
p149tl – Ito & Katy Marks
p149tr – Ito & Katy Marks
p149m – Ito & Katy Marks
p149b – Ito & Katy Marks

**ZHONGSHAN SHIPYARD
PARK**
All images: Turenscape

ESSAY 5
p156 – Dominic Papa
p158 – Dominic Papa
p159 – Dominic Papa
p162 – Sarah Gaventa
p163 – Sarah Gaventa

MUR ISLAND
p164 – Acconci Studio
p165 – Acconci Studio
p166t – Acconci Studio
p166bl – Acconci Studio
p166br – Acconci Studio
p167 – Acconci Studio

SERPENTINE PAVILIONS
p168t – Helene Binet
p168m – Helene Binet
p168b – Helene Binet
p169l – Helene Binet
p169r – Helene Binet
p170tl – Dafydd Jones
p170tr – Dafydd Jones
p171t – Stephen White

p171m – Stephen White
p171b – Stephen White

GREEN GREEN SCREEN
All photographs courtesy Klein
   Dytham

THE HARBOUR POOL
p176 – Photogaphy/Copyright:
   Julien De Smedt
p177t – Photogaphy/Copyright:
   Julien De Smedt
p177b – Photogaphy/Copyright:
   Julien De Smedt
p178 – Casper Dalhoff
p179t – Photogaphy/Copyright:
   Julien De Smedt
p179b – Photogaphy/Copyright:
   Julien De Smedt

MARITIME YOUTH CENTRE
p180–181t –
   Photogaphy/Copyright:
   Julien De Smedt
p180b – Photogaphy/Copyright:
   Julien De Smedt
p181 – Paolo Rosselli
p182t – Photogaphy/Copyright:
   Julien De Smedt
p182b – Mads Hilmer
p183t – Photogaphy/Copyright:
   Julien De Smedt
p183m – Photography/
   Copyright: Julien De Smedt
p183b – Mads Hilmer

ATLANTIC ROAD
p185 – All 3RW Architects

GUERILLA GARDENING
p188 – Dave Meslin
p189t – Dave Meslin
p189bl – Dave Meslin
p189br – Jess Brouse
p189b – Jess Brouse

GREYWORLD
p190t – Greyworld
p190b – Greyworld
p191 – Greyworld
p192t – Bauman Lyons
   Associates
p192b – Greyworld
p192/193 – Greyworld

ACKNOWLEDGMENTS

I would like to thank all those architects, designers, artists, and others involved in the projects featured in the book for giving me their time, information, and views. Also CABE Space and the Concrete Centre for supporting the project. At Mitchell Beazley I would like to thank Peter Taylor and Hannah Barnes-Murphy. Likewise, my partner at Scarlet Projects, Claire Catterall, and finally Dominic Papa and little Raphael Papa, whose early delivery coincided with that of this book.

The **Concrete** Centre